LearningExpress Skill Builders Practice

501
CHALLENGING
LOGIC AND
REASONING
PROBLEMS

ISBN 1-57685-285-7

Printed in the United States of America
9 8 7 6 5
First Edition

For Further Information

For information on LearningExpress, other LearningExpress products, or bulk sales, please write to us at:

LearningExpress™
55 Broadway
8th Floor
New York, NY 10006

Or visit us at:
www.learnatest.com

SKILL BUILDERS PRACTICE TITLES ARE THE PERFECT COMPANIONS TO OUR SKILL BUILDERS BOOKS.

Reading Comprehension Success, 2nd Edition	ISBN 1–57685–126–5
Vocabulary and Spelling Success, 2nd Edition	ISBN 1–57685–127–3
Reasoning Skills Success	ISBN 1–57685–116–8
Writing Skills Success, 2nd Edition	ISBN 1–57685–128–1
Practical Math Success, 2nd Edition	ISBN 1–57685–129–X

What people are saying about LearningExpress Skill Builders...

"Works perfectly! ...an excellent program for preparing students for success on the new Regent's Exam. I love the format, as well as the tips on active reading and study skills. And the pre- and post-tests help me in assessing my class's reading abilities."

— Betty Hodge, 11th Grade English Teacher, Lancaster High School, NY

"The book provides help—help with understanding—for learners seeking to increase their vocabularies and improve their spelling."

—Rose C. Lobat, Jewish Community Center of Staten Island, NY

"I love this book! It is easy to use and extremely user-friendly, and the end results are outstanding."

—Janelle Mason

"If you are still dangling your participles, watching your sentences run on, and feeling irregular about verbs, check out this book. Recommended for the school, workplace, or even home for handy reference."

—Julie Pfeiffer, Middletown Public Library

"I used Writing Skills Success and Practical Math Success in my JTPA classes. They're excellent, concise tools and offered quick, precise ways to get the basics across."

—R. Eddington, JTPA Program Director

CONTENTS

INTRODUCTION

This book—which can be used alone, along with other logic and reasoning texts of your choice, or in combination with the LearningExpress publication, *Reasoning Skills Success in 20 Minutes a Day*—will give you practice dealing with the types of multiple-choice questions that appear on standardized tests assessing logic, reasoning, judgment, and critical thinking. It is designed to be used by individuals working on their own and by teachers or tutors helping students to learn, review, or practice working on basic logic and reasoning skills. Practice on 501 logic and reasoning questions should go a long way in alleviating test anxiety, too!

Maybe you're one of the millions of people who, as students in elementary or high school, never understood the necessity of having to read opinion essays and draw conclusions from the writer's argument. Or maybe you never understood why you had to work through all those verbal analogies or number-series questions. Maybe you were one of those people who could never see a "plan of attack" when working through logic games or critical-thinking puzzles. Or perhaps you could never see a connection between everyday life and analyzing evidence from a series of tedious reading passages. If you fit into one of these groups, this book is for you.

First, know you are not alone. It is true that some people relate more easily than do others to number-series questions, verbal analogies, logic games, and reading passages that present an argument. And that's okay; we all have unique talents. Still, it's a fact that on most jobs today, critical-thinking skills—including analytical and logical reasoning—are essential. The good news is that these skills can be developed with practice.

Learn by doing. It's an old lesson, tried and true. And it's the tool this book is designed to give you. The 501 logic and reasoning questions in this book will provide you with lots of practice. As you work through each set of questions, you'll be gaining a solid understanding of basic analytical and logical reasoning skills. And all without memorizing! The purpose of this book is to help you improve your critical thinking through encouragement, not frustration.

AN OVERVIEW

501 Challenging Logic and Reasoning Problems is divided into 37 sets of questions:

- Sets 1–4: Number Series
- Sets 5–6: Letter and Symbol Series
- Sets 7–8: Verbal Classification
- Sets 9–11: "Essential" Part
- Sets 12–17: Analogies
- Sets 18–19: Artificial Language
- Set 20: Matching Definitions
- Set 21: Making Judgments
- Set 22: Verbal Reasoning
- Sets 23–27: Logic Problems
- Sets 28–31: Logic Games
- Sets 32–37: Analyzing Arguments

Each set contains between eight and twenty questions, depending on their length and difficulty. The book is specifically organized to help you build confidence as you further develop your logic and reasoning skills. *501 Challenging Logic and Reasoning Problems* begins with basic number and letter series questions, and then moves on to verbal-classification, artificial-language, and matching-definition items. The last sets contain logic problems, logic games, and logical reasoning questions. By the time you reach the last question, you'll feel confident that you've improved your critical-thinking and logical-reasoning abilities.

HOW TO USE THIS BOOK

Whether you're working alone or helping someone brush up critical thinking and reasoning skills, this book will give you the opportunity to practice, practice, practice.

WORKING ON YOUR OWN

If you are working alone to improve your logic skills or prepare for a test in connection with a job or school, you will probably want to use this book in combination with its companion text, *Reasoning Skills Success in 20 Minutes a Day*, or with some other basic reasoning skills text. If you're fairly sure of your basic logic and reasoning abilities, however, you can use *501 Challenging Logic and Reasoning Problems* by itself.

Use the answer key at the end of the book not only to find out if you got the right answer, but also to learn how to tackle similar kinds of questions next time. Every answer is explained. Make sure you understand the explanations—usually by going back to the questions—before moving on to the next set.

TUTORING OTHERS

This book will work well in combination with almost any analytical reasoning or logic text. You will probably find it most helpful to give students a brief lesson in the particular operation they'll be learning—number series, verbal classification, artificial language, logic problems, analyzing arguments—and then have them spend the remainder of the session actually answering the questions in the sets. You will want to impress upon them the importance of learning by doing and of checking their answers and reading the explanations carefully. Make sure they understand a particular set of questions before you assign the next one.

ADDITIONAL RESOURCES

Answering the 501 logic and reasoning questions in this book will give you lots of practice. Another way to improve you reasoning ability is to read and study on your own and devise your own unique methods of "attacking" logic problems. Following is a list of logic and reasoning books you may want to buy or take out of the library:

REASONING

Reasoning Skills Success in 20 Minutes a Day by Elizabeth Chesla (LearningExpress)

Analytical Reading and Reasoning by Arthur Whimbey (Innovative Sciences)

What If—: Toward Excellence in Reasoning by Jaakko Hinitkka and James Bachman (Mayfield)

Attacking Faulty Reasoning: A Practical Guide to Fallacy-Free Arguments by T. Edward Danner (Wadsworth)

Thinking Critically: Techniques for Logical Reasoning by James Hugh Kiersky and Nicholas J. Caste (West/Wadsworth)

LOGIC

Essential Logic: Basic Reasoning Skills for the Twenty-first Century by Ronald C. Pine (Harcourt)

Arguments: Deductive Logic Exercises by Howard Pospesel (Prentice Hall)

Increase Your Puzzle IQ: Tips and Tricks for Building Your Logic Power by Marcel Danesi (Wiley)

Amazing Logic Puzzles by Norman D. Willis (Sterling)

CRITICAL THINKING

Brainplay: Challenging Puzzles & Thinking Games by Tom Werneck and Annette Englander (Sterling)

Challenging Critical Thinking Puzzles by Michael A. Dispezio and Myron Miller (Sterling)

Becoming a Critical Thinker: A User-Friendly Manual by Sherry Diestler (Prentice Hall)

Critical Thinking: Step by Step by Robert Cogan
   (University Press of America)

ANALOGIES

Analogies for Beginners by Lynne Chatham (Dandy
   Lion Publications)
Cracking the Miller Analogies Test (2nd Edition)
   by Marcia Lerner (Princeton Review)
Miller Analogies Test: Preparation Guide (2nd
   Edition*)* by Michele Spence (Cliffs Notes)

QUESTIONS

Ready to test your mental abilities? Your *501 Challenging Logic and Reasoning Problems* begin on the next page. They're grouped together in sets of 5–20 questions with a common theme. You can work through the sets in order or jump around, as you choose. When you finish a set, check your answers beginning on page 113.

SET 1 (Answers begin on page 113.)

Start off with these simple series of numbers. Number series questions measure your ability to reason without words. To answer these questions you must determine the pattern of the numbers in each series before you will be able to choose which number comes next. These questions involve only simple arithmetic. Although most number series items progress by adding or subtracting, some questions involve simple multiplication or division. In each series, look for the degree and direction of change between the numbers. In other words, do the numbers increase or decrease, and by how much?

1. Look at this series: 3, 6, 9, 12, 15, . . . What number should come next?
   a. 16
   b. 18
   c. 19
   d. 21

2. Look at this series: 66, 59, 52, 45, 38, . . . What number should come next?
   a. 31
   b. 32
   c. 35
   d. 41

3. Look at this series: 44, 44, 50, 50, 56, . . . What number should come next?
   a. 44
   b. 48
   c. 56
   d. 62

4. Look at this series: 102, 103, 105, 108, . . . What number should come next?
   a. 106
   b. 109
   c. 111
   d. 112

5. Look at this series: 567, 542, 517, 492, . . . What number should come next?
   a. 467
   b. 477
   c. 483
   d. 499

6. Look at this series: 50, 5, 40, 10, 30, . . . What number should come next?
   a. 15
   b. 20
   c. 25
   d. 35

7. Look at this series: 9, 24, 9, 30, 9, . . . What number should come next?
   a. 10
   b. 16
   c. 31
   d. 36

8. Look at this series: 33, 31, 27, 25, 21, . . . What number should come next?
   a. 17
   b. 19
   c. 20
   d. 24

9. Look at this series: 29, 27, 28, 26, 27, 25, . . . What number should come next?
   a. 23
   b. 24
   c. 26
   d. 27

10. Look at this series: 3, 4, 7, 8, 11, 12, . . . What number should come next?

a. 7

b. 10

c. 14

d. 15

11. Look at this series: 31, 29, 24, 22, 17, . . . What number should come next?

a. 15

b. 14

c. 13

d. 12

12. Look at this series: 21, 9, 21, 11, 21, 13, . . . What number should come next?

a. 14

b. 15

c. 21

d. 23

13. Look at this series: 53, 53, 40, 40, 27, 27, . . . What number should come next?

a. 12

b. 14

c. 27

d. 53

14. Look at this series: 2, 6, 18, 54, . . . What number should come next?

a. 108

b. 148

c. 162

d. 216

15. Look at this series: 1000, 200, 40, . . . What number should come next?

a. 8

b. 10

c. 15

d. 20

16. Look at this series: 7, 10, 8, 11, 9, 12, . . . What number should come next?

a. 7

b. 10

c. 12

d. 13

17. Look at this series: 14, 28, 20, 40, 32, 64, . . . What number should come next?

a. 52

b. 56

c. 96

d. 128

18. Look at this series: 1.5, 2.3, 3.1, 3.9, . . . What number should come next?

a. 4.2

b. 4.4

c. 4.7

d. 5.1

19. Look at this series: 5.2, 4.8, 4.4, 4, . . . What number should come next?

a. 3

b. 3.3

c. 3.5

d. 3.6

20. Look at this series: 2, 1, ½, ¼, . . . What number should come next?

a. ⅓

b. ⅛

c. ⅜

d. ¹⁄₁₆

SET 2 (Answers begin on page 115.)

This set contains additional, and sometimes more difficult, number series questions. Again, each question has a definite pattern. Some of the number series may be interrupted by a particular number that appears periodically in the pattern. For example, in the series 14, 16, 32, 18, 20, 32, 22, 24, 32, the number 32 appears as every third number. Sometimes the pattern contains two alternating series. For example, in the series 1, 5, 3, 7, 5, 9, 7, the pattern is add 4, subtract 2, add 4, subtract 2, and so on. Look carefully for the pattern, and then choose which *pair* of numbers comes next. Note also that you will be choosing from 5 options instead of 4.

21. 74 66 58 50 42 34 26
   a. 20 12
   b. 18 8
   c. 20 10
   d. 18 10
   e. 16 8

22. 2 7 12 17 22 27 32
   a. 38 42
   b. 37 42
   c. 37 43
   d. 36 42
   e. 32 37

23. 19 19 17 17 15 15 13
   a. 11 11
   b. 13 13
   c. 13 15
   d. 11 12
   e. 13 11

24. 21 24 30 21 36 42 21
   a. 54 21
   b. 50 56
   c. 48 21
   d. 46 54
   e. 48 54

25. 9 11 33 13 15 33 17
   a. 19 33
   b. 33 35
   c. 33 19
   d. 15 33
   e. 19 21

26. 2 8 14 20 26 32 38
   a. 2 46
   b. 44 50
   c. 42 48
   d. 40 42
   e. 32 26

27. 28 25 5 21 18 5 14
   a. 11 5
   b. 10 7
   c. 11 8
   d. 5 10
   e. 10 5

28. 9 12 11 14 13 16 15
   a. 14 13
   b. 18 21
   c. 14 17
   d. 12 13
   e. 18 17

29. 75 65 85 55 45 85 35
   a. 25 15
   b. 25 85
   c. 35 25
   d. 85 35
   e. 25 75

30. 1 10 7 20 13 30 19
   a. 26 40
   b. 29 36
   c. 40 25
   d. 25 31
   e. 40 50

31. 10 20 25 35 40 50 55
   a. 70 65
   b. 60 70
   c. 60 75
   d. 60 65
   e. 65 70

32. 40 40 31 31 22 22 13
   a. 13 4
   b. 13 5
   c. 4 13
   d. 9 4
   e. 4 4

33. 17 17 34 20 20 31 23
   a. 26 23
   b. 34 20
   c. 23 33
   d. 27 28
   e. 23 28

34. 2 3 4 5 6 4 8
   a. 9 10
   b. 4 8
   c. 10 4
   d. 9 4
   e. 8 9

35. 61 57 50 61 43 36 61
   a. 29 61
   b. 27 20
   c. 31 61
   d. 22 15
   e. 29 22

36. 9 16 23 30 37 44 51
   a. 59 66
   b. 56 62
   c. 58 66
   d. 58 65
   e. 54 61

37. 8 22 12 16 22 20 24
   a. 28 32
   b. 28 22
   c. 22 28
   d. 32 36
   e. 22 26

38. 2 22 4 18 6 14 8
   a. 10 12
   b. 10 6
   c. 12 8
   d. 10 10
   e. 18 6

39. 13 17 21 25 29 33 37
   a. 42 46
   b. 41 46
   c. 42 47
   d. 41 45
   e. 41 55

40. 7 10 19 14 17 19 21
   a. 24 17
   b. 24 19
   c. 24 27
   d. 25 28
   e. 19 22

SET 3 (Answers begin on page 117.)

This set will give you additional practice dealing with number series questions.

41. 44 41 38 35 32 29 26
  a. 24 21
  b. 22 19
  c. 23 19
  d. 29 32
  e. 23 20

42. 6 10 14 18 22 26 30
  a. 36 40
  b. 33 37
  c. 38 42
  d. 34 36
  e. 34 38

43. 34 30 26 22 18 14 10
  a. 8 6
  b. 6 4
  c. 14 18
  d. 6 2
  e. 4 0

44. 2 44 4 41 6 38 8
  a. 10 12
  b. 35 32
  c. 34 9
  d. 35 10
  e. 10 52

45. 32 29 26 23 20 17 14
  a. 11 8
  b. 12 8
  c. 11 7
  d. 32 29
  e. 10 9

46. 17 17 28 28 39 39 50
  a. 60 71
  b. 50 61
  c. 50 71
  d. 61 72
  e. 50 62

47. 7 12 9 14 11 16 13
  a. 16 13
  b. 18 15
  c. 10 15
  d. 18 23
  e. 10 7

48. 2 5 28 8 11 20 14
  a. 12 4
  b. 12 17
  c. 18 12
  d. 17 6
  e. 17 12

49. 4 9 11 16 18 23 25
  a. 27 29
  b. 30 35
  c. 30 32
  d. 27 32
  e. 27 30

50. 17 14 14 11 11 8 8
  a. 8 5
  b. 5 2
  c. 8 2
  d. 5 5
  e. 5 8

51. 13 29 15 26 17 23 19
  a. 21 23
  b. 20 21
  c. 20 17
  d. 25 27
  e. 22 20

52. 16 26 56 36 46 68 56
a. 80 66
b. 64 82
c. 66 80
d. 78 68
e. 66 82

53. 7 9 66 12 14 66 17
a. 19 66
b. 66 19
c. 19 22
d. 20 66
e. 66 20

54. 3 5 35 10 12 35 17
a. 22 35
b. 35 19
c. 19 35
d. 19 24
e. 22 24

55. 36 31 29 24 22 17 15
a. 13 11
b. 10 5
d. 13 8
d. 12 7
e. 10 8

56. 42 40 38 35 33 31 28
a. 25 22
b. 26 23
c. 26 24
d. 25 23
e. 26 22

57. 11 14 14 17 17 20 20
a. 23 23
b. 23 26
c. 21 24
d. 24 24
e. 24 27

58. 17 32 19 29 21 26 23
a. 25 25
b. 20 22
c. 23 25
d. 25 22
e. 27 32

59. 10 34 12 31 14 28 16
a. 25 18
b. 30 13
c. 19 26
d. 18 20
e. 25 22

60. 32 31 32 29 32 27 32
a. 25 32
b. 31 32
c. 29 32
d. 25 30
e. 29 30

SET 4 (Answers begin on page 118.)

This set contains additional number series questions, some of which are in Roman numerals. These items are different from Sets 1, 2, and 3, because they ask you to find the number that fits somewhere into the *middle* of the series. Some of the items involve both numbers and letters; for these questions, look for a number series *and* a letter series. (For additional practice in working letter series questions, see Set 5.)

61. Look at this series: 10, 34, 12, 31, __, 28, 16,
. . . What number should fill the blank?
a. 14
b. 18
c. 30
d. 34

62. Look at this series: 17, __, 28, 28, 39, 39, . . .
What number should fill the blank?
a. 50
b. 39
c. 25
d. 17

63. Look at this series: 75, 65, 85, 55, __, 85, 35,
. . . What number should fill the blank?
a. 25
b. 45
c. 65
d. 85

64. Look at this series: 2, 5, 28, 8, __, 20, 14, 17
. . . What number should fill the blank?
a. 11
b. 17
c. 20
d. 28

65. Look at this series: 84, 89, 86, 91, 88, __, 90,
. . . What number should fill the blank?
a. 83
b. 85
c. 92
d. 93

66. Look at this series: 70, 71, 76, __, 81, 86, 70,
91, . . . What number should fill the blank?
a. 70
b. 71
c. 80
d. 96

67. Look at this series: 664, 332, 340, 170, __, 89,
. . . What number should fill the blank?
a. 85
b. 97
c. 109
d. 178

68. Look at this series: 0.15, 0.3, __, 1.2, 2.4, . . .
What number should fill the blank?
a. 4.8
b. 0.006
c. 0.6
d. 0.9

69. Look at this series: ⅑, ⅓, 1, __, 9, . . . What
number should fill the blank?
a. ⅔
b. 3
c. 6
d. 27

70. Look at this series: U32, V29, __, X23, Y20,
. . . What number should fill the blank?
a. W26
b. W17
c. Z17
d. Z26

71. Look at this series: J14, L16, __, P20, R22, . . .
    What number should fill the blank?
    a. S24
    b. N18
    c. M18
    d. T24

72. Look at this series: F2, __, D8, C16, B32, . . .
    What number should fill the blank?
    a. A16
    b. G4
    c. E4
    d. E3

73. Look at this series: V, VIII, XI, XIV, __, XX,
    . . . What number should fill the blank?
    a. IX
    b. XXIII
    c. XV
    d. XVII

74. Look at this series: XXIV, XX, __, XII, VIII,
    . . . What number should fill the blank?
    a. XXII
    b. XIII
    c. XVI
    d. IV

75. Look at this series: VI, 10, V, 11, __, 12, III,
    . . . What number should fill the blank?
    a. II
    b. IV
    c. IX
    d. 14

SET 5 (Answers begin on page 119.)

Another type of sequence question involves a series of letters in a pattern. Usually these questions use the letters' alphabetical order as a base. To make matters more complicated, sometimes subscript numbers will be thrown into the letter sequence. In these series, you will be looking at both the letter pattern and the number pattern. Some of these questions ask you to fill the blank in the middle of the series; others ask you to add to the end of the series.

76. QPO NML KJI _____ EDC
   a. HGF
   b. CAB
   c. JKL
   d. GHI

77. JAK KBL LCM MDN _____
   a. OEP
   b. NEO
   c. MEN
   d. PFQ

78. B_2CD _____ BCD_4 B_5CD BC_6D
   a. B_2C_2D
   b. BC_3D
   c. B_2C_3D
   d. BCD_7

79. ELFA GLHA ILJA _____ MLNA
   a. OLPA
   b. KLMA
   c. LLMA
   d. KLLA

80. P_5QR P_4QS P_3QT _____ PQV
   a. PQW
   b. PQV_2
   c. P_2QU
   d. PQ_3U

81. CMM EOO GQQ _____ KUU
   a. GRR
   b. GSS
   c. ISS
   d. ITT

82. QAR RAS SAT TAU _____
   a. UAV
   b. UAT
   c. TAS
   d. TAT

83. DEF DEF_2 DE_2F_2 _____ $D_2E_2F_3$
   a. DEF_3
   b. D_3EF_3
   c. D_2E_3F
   d. $D_2E_2F_2$

84. VAB WCD XEF _____ ZIJ
   a. AKL
   b. UHG
   c. YGH
   d. GHW

85. BOC COB DOE EOD _____
   a. FOG
   b. DOG
   c. DOF
   d. FOE

86. LML NON PQP RSR _____
   a. TUT
   b. RTR
   c. STS
   d. TRT

87. ZA_5 Y_4B XC_6 W_3D _____
   a. E_7V
   b. V_2E
   c. VE_5
   d. VE_7

SET 6 (Answers begin on page 120.)

This set contains sequence questions that use a series of nonverbal, non-number symbols. Look carefully at the sequence of symbols to find the pattern.

88.

⇨⇨ | ⇧⇩ | ⇨⇨ | ⇧⇩ —

⇩⇩ ⇨⇨ ⇩⇧ ⇦⇦
a.   b.   c.   d.

89.

o ◯ ● | ▲ △ △ | ▢ —

▢▢ ▢■ △▲ ▢■
a.   b.   c.   d.

90.

Ε π Ε | π π π | Ε ω Ε | ω _ ω

π Ε ω Ξ
a. b. c. d.

91.

⊙◉● | ⊙⊙◯ | ●◉ —

● ◉ ⊙ ◯
a. b. c. d.

92.

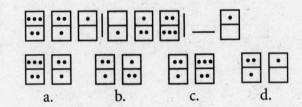

a.   b.   c.   d.

93.

a.   b.   c.   d.

94.

▢◯ ▢△ | ⌂ ▯ | ◉ ▢△ | ▯ —

⌂ ⌂ ▯ ◯
a. b. c. d.

95.

△▢△ | ▢◯▢ | ◯◇◯ | ◇▢ —

◇ ▭ ◯ △
a. b. c. d.

96.

↑ ↗ → ↘ ↓ ↙ —

↖ ← ↑ ↔
a. b. c. d.

97.

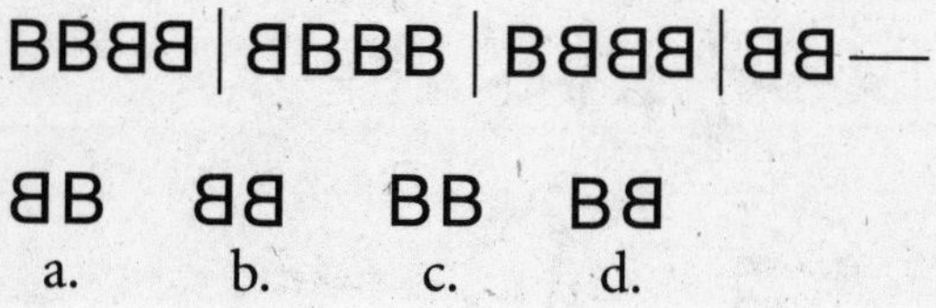

98.

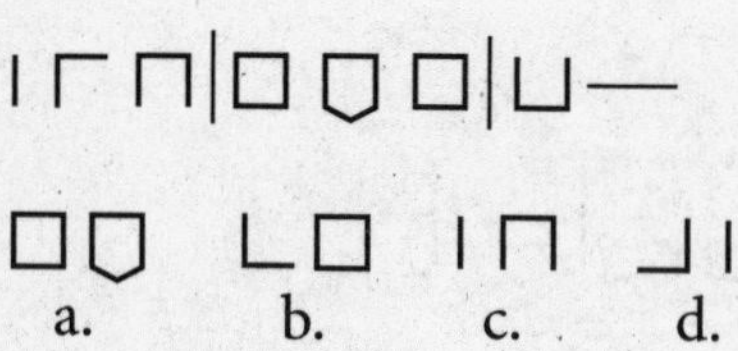

99.

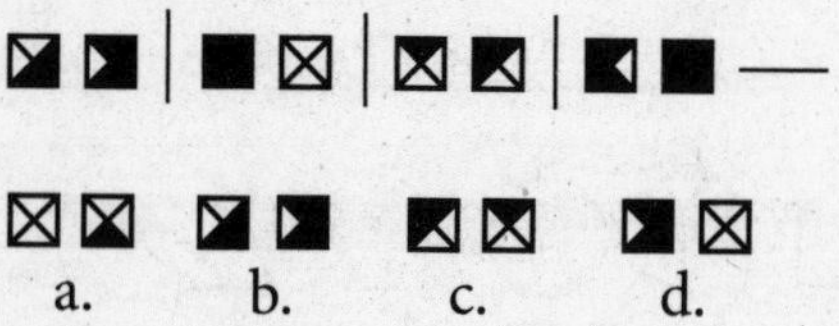

100.

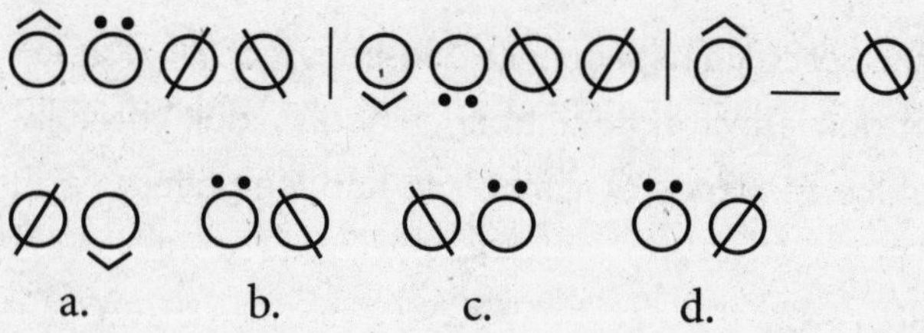

101.

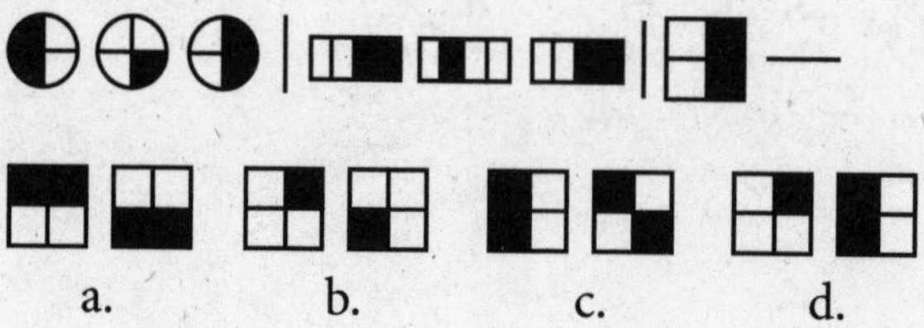

SET 7 (Answers begin on page 122.)

The next two sets contain verbal classification questions. For these questions, the important thing (as the name "verbal classification" indicates) is to *classify* the words in the four answer choices. Three of the words will be in the same classification; the remaining one will not be. Your answer will be the one word that does *not* belong in the same classification as the others.

102. Which word does NOT belong with the others?
    a. leopard
    b. cougar
    c. elephant
    d. lion

103. Which word does NOT belong with the others?
    a. couch
    b. rug
    c. table
    d. chair

104. Which word does NOT belong with the others?
    a. tape
    b. twine
    c. cord
    d. yarn

105. Which word does NOT belong with the others?
    a. flute
    b. violin
    c. saxophone
    d. trumpet

106. Which word does NOT belong with the others?
    a. sleeve
    b. pocket
    c. collar
    d. shirt

107. Which word does NOT belong with the others?
    a. pecan
    b. walnut
    c. kernel
    d. cashew

108. Which word does NOT belong with the others?
    a. rayon
    b. silk
    c. cotton
    d. cloth

109. Which word does NOT belong with the others?
    a. roof
    b. sidewalk
    c. door
    d. window

110. Which word does NOT belong with the others?
    a. unimportant
    b. trivial
    c. insignificant
    d. familiar

111. Which word does NOT belong with the others?
a. book
b. index
c. glossary
d. chapter

112. Which word does NOT belong with the others?
a. noun
b. preposition
c. punctuation
d. adverb

113. Which word does NOT belong with the others?
a. cornea
b. retina
c. pupil
d. vision

114. Which word does NOT belong with the others?
a. rye
b. sourdough
c. pumpernickel
d. loaf

115. Which word does NOT belong with the others?
a. inch
b. ounce
c. centimeter
d. yard

116. Which word does NOT belong with the others?
a. street
b. freeway
c. interstate
d. expressway

117. Which word does NOT belong with the others?
a. dodge
b. flee
c. duck
d. avoid

118. Which word does NOT belong with the others?
a. heading
b. body
c. letter
d. closing

SET 8 (Answers begin on page 123.)

Here's another set of classification questions. Remember that you are looking for the word that does *not* belong in the same group as the others. Sometimes, all four words seem to fit the same group. If so, you must look more closely to further narrow your classification.

119. Which word does NOT belong with the others?
    a. core
    b. seeds
    c. pulp
    d. slice

120. Which word does NOT belong with the others?
    a. festive
    b. lucky
    c. joyous
    d. merry

121. Which word does NOT belong with the others?
    a. geology
    b. zoology
    c. theology
    d. botany

122. Which word does NOT belong with the others?
    a. sphere
    b. parallelogram
    c. square
    d. rectangle

123. Which word does NOT belong with the others?
    a. baffle
    b. falter
    c. hesitate
    d. waver

124. Which word does NOT belong with the others?
    a. instruct
    b. teach
    c. educate
    d. discipline

125. Which word does NOT belong with the others?
    a. lobster
    b. trout
    c. sardine
    b. catfish

126. Which word does NOT belong with the others?
    a. scythe
    b. knife
    c. pliers
    d. saw

127. Which word does NOT belong with the others?
    a. two
    b. three
    c. six
    d. eight

128. Which word does NOT belong with the others?
    a. peninsula
    b. island
    c. bay
    d. cape

129. Which word does NOT belong with the others?
a. seat
b. rung
c. cushion
d. leg

130. Which word does NOT belong with the others?
a. fair
b. just
c. equitable
d. favorable

131. Which word does NOT belong with the others?
a. defendant
b. prosecutor
c. trial
d. judge

132. Which word does NOT belong with the others?
a. area
b. variable
c. circumference
d. quadrilateral

133. Which word does NOT belong with the others?
a. mayor
b. lawyer
c. governor
d. senator

134. Which word does NOT belong with the others?
a. acute
b. right
c. obtuse
d. parallel

135. Which word does NOT belong with the others?
a. wing
b. fin
c. beak
d. rudder

136. Which word does NOT belong with the others?
a. aorta
b. heart
c. liver
d. stomach

SET 9 (Answers begin on page 124.)

In the next three sets, you will be looking for the essential part of something. Each question has an underlined word followed by four answer choices. You will choose the word that is a *necessary* part of the underlined word. A good way to approach this type of question is to say the following sentence: "A _____ could not exist without _____." Put the underlined word in the first blank. Try each of the answer choices in the second blank to see which choice is most logical.

For Questions 137 through 151, find the word that names a *necessary* part of the underlined word.

137. book
    a. fiction
    b. pages
    c. pictures
    d. learning

138. piano
    a. orchestra
    b. notes
    c. teacher
    d. keyboard

139. shoe
    a. sole
    b. leather
    c. laces
    d. walking

140. respiration
    a. mouth
    b. circulation
    c. oxygen
    d. carbon monoxide

141. election
    a. president
    b. voter
    c. November
    d. nation

142. diploma
    a. principal
    b. curriculum
    c. employment
    d. graduation

143. lake
    a. boats
    b. swimming
    c. water
    d. beach

144. army
    a. soldiers
    b. navy
    c. war
    d. training

145. language
    a. tongue
    b. slang
    c. writing
    d. words

146. desert
    a. cactus
    b. arid
    c. oasis
    d. flat

147. lightning
    a. electricity
    b. thunder
    c. brightness
    d. rain

148. <u>monopoly</u>
   a. corrupt
   b. exclusive
   c. rich
   d. gigantic

149. <u>harvest</u>
   a. autumn
   b. stockpile
   c. tractor
   d. crop

150. <u>gala</u>
   a. celebration
   b. tuxedo
   c. appetizer
   d. orator

151. <u>pain</u>
   a. cut
   b. burn
   c. nuisance
   d. hurt

SET 10 (Answers begin on page 125.)

Remember that you are looking for the essential part of something. If you had trouble working Set 9, go back through the items and study each answer explanation. Then work through this set of more difficult necessary-part questions.

For Questions 152 through 166, find the word that names a *necessary* part of the underlined word.

152. infirmary
   a. surgery
   b. disease
   c. patient
   d. receptionist

153. facsimile
   a. picture
   b. image
   c. mimeograph
   d. copier

154. domicile
   a. tenant
   b. dwelling
   c. kitchen
   d. house

155. culture
   a. civility
   b. education
   c. agriculture
   d. customs

156. bonus
   a. reward
   b. raise
   c. cash
   d. employer

157. antique
   a. rarity
   b. artifact
   c. aged
   d. prehistoric

158. itinerary
   a. map
   b. route
   c. travel
   d. guidebook

159. orchestra
   a. violin
   b. stage
   c. musician
   d. soloist

160. knowledge
   a. school
   b. teacher
   c. textbook
   d. learning

161. dimension
   a. compass
   b. ruler
   c. inch
   d. measure

162. sustenance
   a. nourishment
   b. water
   c. grains
   d. menu

163. ovation
   a. outburst
   b. bravo
   c. applause
   d. encore

164. <u>vertebrate</u>
   a. backbone
   b. reptile
   c. mammal
   d. animal

165. <u>provisions</u>
   a. groceries
   b. supplies
   c. gear
   d. caterers

166. <u>purchase</u>
   a. trade
   b. money
   c. bank
   d. acquisition

SET 11 (Answers begin on page 127.)

Here is one more set of necessary-part questions. This set is somewhat more difficult than the previous two sets, and it should give you practice in mastering this particular type of question. Remember that a good way to approach this type of question is to use the following sentence: "A _____ could not exist without _____."

For Questions 167 through 181, find the word that names a *necessary* part of the underlined word.

167. <u>dome</u>
    a. rounded
    b. geodesic
    c. governmental
    d. coppery

168. <u>recipe</u>
    a. food
    b. directions
    c. cookbook
    d. utensils

169. <u>hurricane</u>
    a. beach
    b. cyclone
    c. damage
    d. wind

170. <u>autograph</u>
    a. athlete
    b. actor
    c. signature
    d. pen

171. <u>town</u>
    a. residents
    b. skyscrapers
    c. parks
    d. libraries

172. <u>wedding</u>
    a. love
    b. church
    c. ring
    d. marriage

173. <u>faculty</u>
    a. buildings
    b. textbooks
    c. teachers
    d. meetings

174. <u>cage</u>
    a. enclosure
    b. prisoner
    c. animal
    d. zoo

175. <u>directory</u>
    a. telephone
    b. listing
    c. computer
    d. names

176. <u>contract</u>
    a. agreement
    b. document
    c. written
    d. attorney

177. <u>saddle</u>
    a. horse
    b. seat
    c. stirrups
    d. horn

178. <u>vibration</u>
   a. motion
   b. electricity
   c. science
   d. sound

179. <u>cell</u>
   a. chlorophyll
   b. nucleus
   c. nerve
   d. human

180. <u>champion</u>
   a. running
   b. swimming
   c. winning
   d. speaking

181. <u>glacier</u>
   a. mountain
   b. winter
   c. prehistory
   d. ice

SET 12 (Answers begin on page 129.)

Here is the first of several sets of analogies. Analogies test your ability to see relationships between words, objects, or concepts. There are many different types of analogy relationships. Some of the possibilities are as follows: use or function, part-to-whole, classification, proportion or degree, cause and effect, similarity or difference. In each of these verbal analogies, you will be given a set of two words that are related, followed by a third word and four answer choices. Of the four choices, you must identify the one that would best complete the second set so that it expresses the same relationship as in the first set. A good way to figure out the relationship in a given question is to make up a sentence that describes the relationship between the first two words. Then try to use the same sentence to find out which of the answer choices completes the same relationship with the third word.

182. Cup is to coffee as bowl is to
   a. dish
   b. soup
   c. spoon
   d. food

183. Communication is to telephone as transportation is to
   a. aviation
   b. travel
   c. information
   d. bus

184. Bicycle is to pedal as canoe is to
   a. water
   b. kayak
   c. oar
   d. fleet

185. Window is to pane as book is to
   a. novel
   b. glass
   c. cover
   d. page

186. Scarcely is to mostly as quietly is to
   a. secretly
   b. rudely
   c. loudly
   d. silently

187. Baker is to bread as congressman is to
   a. senator
   b. law
   c. state
   d. politician

188. Play is to actor as concert is to
   a. symphony
   b. musician
   c. piano
   d. percussion

189. Tactful is to diplomatic as bashful is to
   a. timid
   b. confident
   c. uncomfortable
   d. bold

190. Pride is to lion as school is to
   a. teacher
   b. student
   c. self-respect
   d. fish

191. Control is to dominate as magnify is to
   a. enlarge
   b. preserve
   c. decrease
   d. divide

192. Yard is to inch as quart is to
    a. gallon
    b. ounce
    c. milk
    d. liquid

193. Rodent is to mouse as tree is to
    a. leaf
    b. trunk
    c. elm
    d. squirrel

194. Elated is to despondent as enlightened is to
    a. aware
    b. ignorant
    c. miserable
    d. tolerant

195. Marathon is to race as hibernation is to
    a. winter
    b. bear
    c. dream
    d. sleep

196. Embarrassed is to humiliated as frightened is to
    a. terrified
    b. agitated
    c. courageous
    d. reckless

197. Odometer is to mileage as compass is to
    a. speed
    b. hiking
    c. needle
    d. direction

198. Optimist is to cheerful as pessimist is to
    a. gloomy
    b. mean
    c. petty
    d. helpful

199. Sponge is to porous as rubber is to
    a. massive
    b. solid
    c. elastic
    d. inflexible

200. Candid is to indirect as honest is to
    a. frank
    b. wicked
    c. truthful
    d. untruthful

201. Pen is to poet as needle is to
    a. thread
    b. button
    c. sewing
    d. tailor

SET 13 (Answers begin on page 131.)

Now that you have some practice working basic analogies, try these picture analogies, which will give you practice with nonverbal reasoning. Solve these picture analogies in the same way that you solved the word analogies. For each item, you will be presented with a set of two pictures that are related to each other in the same way. Along with this pair, you'll be given a third picture and four answer choices, which are also pictures. Of the four choices, choose the picture that would go in the empty box so that the two bottom pictures are related in the same way as the top two are related.

203.

a.   b.   c.   d.

202.

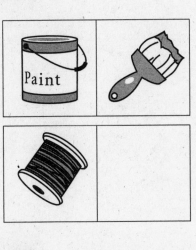

a.   b.   c.   d.

204.

a.   b.   c.   d.

205.

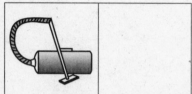

a.　　b.　　c.　　d.

206.

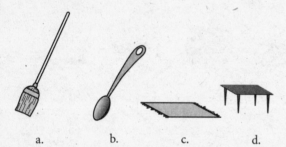

a.　　b.　　c.　　d.

207.

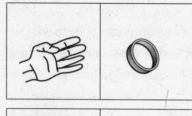

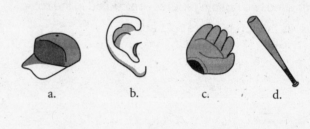

a.　　b.　　c.　　d.

208.

a.　　b.　　c.　　d.

209.

a.

b.

c.

d.

210.

a.

b.

c.

d.

211.

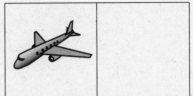

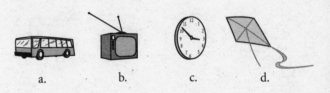

a.

b.

c.

d.

212.

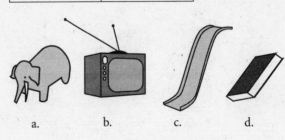

a.

b.

c.

d.

213.

a.   b.   c.   d.

214.

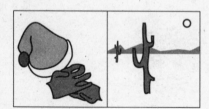

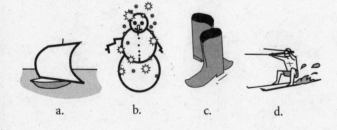

a.   b.   c.   d.

215.

a.   b.   c.   d.

216.

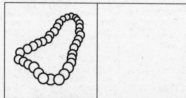

a.   b.   c.   d.

217.

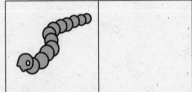

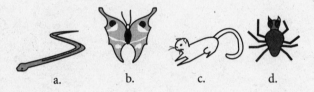

a. b. c. d.

218.

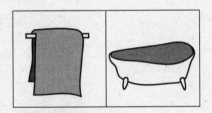

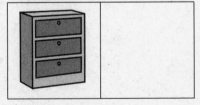

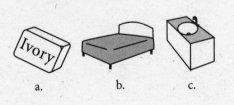

a. b. c. d.

219.

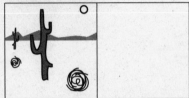

a. b. c. d.

220.

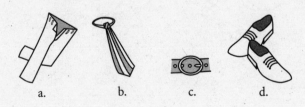

a. b. c. d.

221.

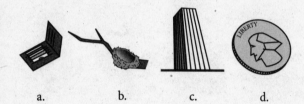

a.   b.   c.   d.

SET 14 (Answers begin on page 133.)

Here are twenty more picture analogies for you to master. There is essentially no difference between verbal and picture analogies, except that you have to take an extra first step by naming each picture. Make sure you understand the relationship between the first set of pictures before you attempt to choose an answer. Make up a sentence that describes this relationship. From the four answer choices, choose the picture that would go in the empty box so that the two bottom pictures are related in the same way as the top two are related.

222.

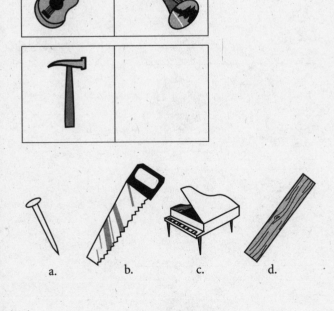

a.   b.   c.   d.

223.

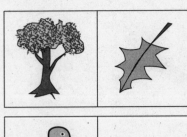

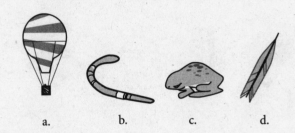

a.   b.   c.   d.

224.

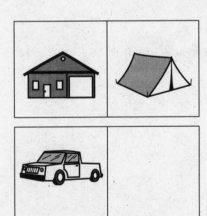

a.   b.   c.   d.

225.

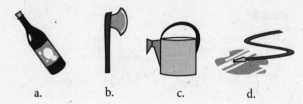

a.　　b.　　c.　　d.

227.

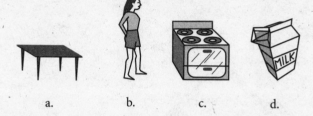

a.　　　　b.　　　　c.　　　　d.

226.

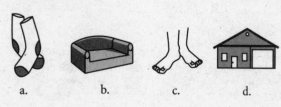

a.　　　　b.　　　　c.　　　　d.

228.

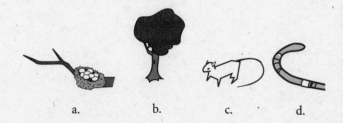

a.　　　　b.　　　　c.　　　　d.

229.

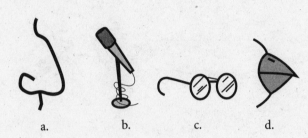

a. b. c. d.

230.

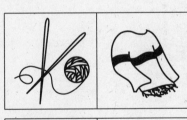

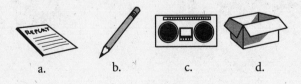

a. b. c. d.

231.

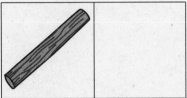

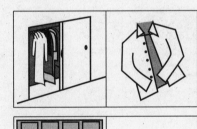

a. b. c. d.

232.

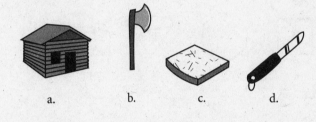

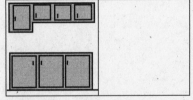

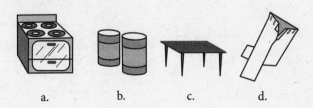

a. b. c. d.

233.

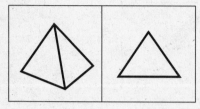

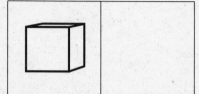

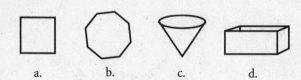

a.   b.   c.   d.

234.

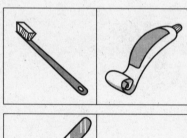

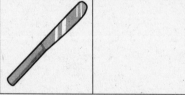

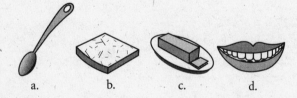

a.   b.   c.   d.

235.

a.   b.   c.   d.

236.

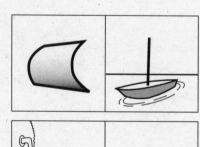

a.   b.   c.   d.

237.

a.   b.   c.   d.

238.

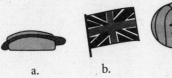

a.   b.   c.   d.

239.

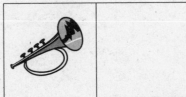

a.   b.   c.   d.

240.

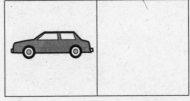

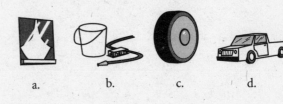

a.   b.   c.   d.

241.

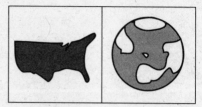

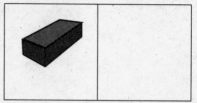

a.   b.   c.   d.

SET 15 (Answers begin on page 135.)

This set contains another type of verbal-analogy questions. In each of these, the words in the top row are related in some way. To help you discover this relationship, make up a sentence based on the top three words. The words in the bottom row are related in the same way as the words in the top row. For each item, find the word that completes the bottom row of words.

242.

ant	fly	bee
hamster	squirrel	_____

   a. spider
   b. mouse
   c. rodent
   d. cat

243.

firefighter	ladder	hose
veterinarian	thermometer	_____

   a. stethoscope
   b. kitten
   c. doctor
   d. injury

244.

table	wood	oak
shirt	cloth	_____

   a. sewing
   b. dress
   c. cotton
   d. tree

245.

rule	command	dictate
doze	sleep	_____

   a. snore
   b. govern
   c. awaken
   d. hibernate

246.

meal	banquet	feast
shelter	palace	_____

   a. mansion
   b. hallway
   c. protection
   d. haven

247.

fence	wall	boundary
path	alley	_____

   a. ramp
   b. passageway
   c. airfield
   d. pedestrian

248.

saw	screwdriver	hammer
spade	hoe	_____

   a. carpenter
   b. gardener
   c. rake
   d. wrench

249.

snow	mountain	ski
warmth	lake	_____

   a. sand
   b. swim
   c. sunburn
   d. vacation

250. candle   lamp   floodlight
hut   cottage   _____
a. tent
b. city
c. dwelling
d. house

251. aspirin   medicine   pharmacy
lettuce   vegetable   _____
a. grocery
b. carrots
c. fruit
d. shopping

252. tadpole   frog   amphibian
lamb   sheep   _____
a. animal
b. wool
c. farm
d. mammal

253. walk   skip   run
toss   pitch   _____
a. swerve
b. hurl
c. jump
d. dance

254. honeybee   angel   bat
kangaroo   rabbit   _____
a. mermaid
b. possum
c. grasshopper
d. sprinter

255. daisy   flower   plant
bungalow   house   _____
a. building
b. cottage
c. apartment
d. city

SET 16 (Answers begin on page 136.)

The next two sets will give you more practice with analogies. Every one of the following questions consists of a related pair of words, followed by five pairs of words labeled A through E. Choose the pair that *best* represents a similar relationship to the one expressed in the original pair of words. Remember, the best way to approach an analogy question is to make up a sentence that describes the relationship between the first two words. Then, find the pair that has a similar relationship.

256. LEAF : TREE
   a. chip : dip
   b. shelf : bookcase
   c. base : ball
   d. curtains : drapes
   e. recliner : chair

257. KEY : PIANO
   a. foot : hand
   b. stage : curtain
   c. bench : chair
   d. brick : wall
   e. frame : portrait

258. WOLF : PACK
   a. lion : pride
   b. antelope : jungle
   c. collie : clan
   d. herd : peacock
   e. raven : school

259. RULER : LENGTH
   a. scale: weight
   b. belt : girth
   c. width : depth
   d. mileage : speed
   e. size : area

260. BROCCOLI : VEGETABLE
   a. type : breed
   b. cat : companion
   c. mark : spot
   d. Dalmatian : canine
   e. collar : leash

261. OAR : CANOE
   a. run : walk
   b. inch : yardstick
   c. tire : automobile
   d. sleeve : shirt
   e. foot : skateboard

262. FRAY : RAVEL
   a. tremble : roll
   b. hungry : eat
   c. jolt : shake
   d. stroll : run
   e. stitch : tear

263. ELEPHANT : PACHYDERM
   a. mantis : rodent
   b. poodle : feline
   c. kangaroo : marsupial
   d. zebra : horse
   e. tuna : mollusk

264. DEPRESSED : SAD
   a. neat : considerate
   b. towering : cringing
   c. rapid : plodding
   d. progressive : regressive
   e. exhausted : tired

265. PSYCHOLOGIST : NEUROSIS
   a. ophthalmologist : cataract
   b. dermatologist : fracture
   c. infant : pediatrician
   d. rash : orthopedist
   e. oncologist : measles

266. BINDING : BOOK
 a. criminal : gang
 b. display : museum
 c. artist : carpenter
 d. nail : hammer
 e. frame : picture

267. EXPLORE : DISCOVER
 a. read : skim
 b. research : learn
 c. write : print
 d. think : relate
 e. sleep : wake

268. COTTON : BALE
 a. butter : churn
 b. wine : ferment
 c. grain : shock
 d. curd : cheese
 e. beef : steak

269. DIVISION : SECTION
 a. layer : tier
 b. tether : bundle
 c. chapter : verse
 d. riser : stage
 e. dais : speaker

270. PASTORAL : RURAL
 a. metropolitan : urban
 b. harvest : autumn
 c. agrarian : benevolent
 d. sleepy : nocturnal
 e. wild : agricultural

271. MECHANIC : GARAGE
 a. teacher : recess
 b. actor : role
 c. jockey : horse
 d. surgeon : hospital
 e. author : book

272. CHICKADEE : BIRD
 a. crocodile : alligator
 b. giraffe : reptile
 c. Siamese : cat
 d. shepherd : marsupial
 e. grasshopper : ant

273. WALK : SAUNTER
 a. trot : race
 b. swim : dive
 c. hop : shuffle
 d. juggle : bounce
 e. rain : drizzle

274. SKEIN : YARN
 a. squeeze : lemon
 b. fire : coal
 c. ream : paper
 d. tree : lumber
 e. plow : acre

275. TAILOR : SUIT
 a. scheme : agent
 b. edit : manuscript
 c. revise : writer
 d. mention : opinion
 e. implode : building

SET 17 (Answers begin on page 137.)

Now try this last set of analogies, which are somewhat more difficult than the previous set. Remember that the first step in solving an analogy is to make up a sentence that describes the relationship between the first two words. Sometimes, your sentence may fit more than one answer choice. In these cases, be prepared to revise your original sentence. Each one of the following questions consists of a related pair of words, followed by five pairs of words labeled A through E. Choose the pair that *best* represents a similar relationship to the one expressed in the original pair of words.

276. CONDUCTOR : ORCHESTRA
  a. jockey : mount
  b. thrasher : hay
  c. driver : tractor
  d. skipper : crew
  e. painter : house

277. JAUNDICE : LIVER
  a. rash : skin
  b. dialysis : kidney
  c. smog : lung
  d. valentine : heart
  e. imagination : brain

278. COBBLER : SHOE
  a. jockey : horse
  b. contractor : building
  c. mason : stone
  d. cowboy : boot
  e. potter : paint

279. PHOBIC : FEARFUL
  a. finicky : thoughtful
  b. cautious : emotional
  c. envious : desiring
  d. shy : familiar
  e. asinine : silly

280. INTEREST : OBSESSION
  a. mood : feeling
  b. weeping : sadness
  c. dream : fantasy
  d. plan : negation
  e. highlight : indication

281. MONK : DEVOTION
  a. maniac : pacifism
  b. explorer : contentment
  c. visionary : complacency
  d. rover : wanderlust
  e. philistine : culture

282. SLAPSTICK : LAUGHTER
  a. fallacy : dismay
  b. genre : mystery
  c. satire : anger
  d. mimicry : tears
  e. horror : fear

283. VERVE : ENTHUSIASM
  a. loyalty : duplicity
  b. devotion : reverence
  c. intensity : color
  d. eminence : anonymity
  e. generosity : elation

284. SOUND : CACOPHONY
  a. taste : style
  b. touch : massage
  c. smell : stench
  d. sight : panorama
  e. speech : oration

285. CONVICTION : INCARCERATION
a. reduction : diminution
b. induction : amelioration
c. radicalization : estimation
d. marginalization : intimidation
e. proliferation : alliteration

286. DELTOID : MUSCLE
a. radius : bone
b. brain : nerve
c. tissue : organ
d. blood : vein
e. scalpel : incision

287. UMBRAGE : OFFENSE
a. confusion : penance
b. infinity : meaning
c. decorum : decoration
d. elation : jubilance
e. outrage : consideration

288. PROFESSOR : ERUDITE
a. aviator : licensed
b. inventor : imaginative
c. procrastinator : conscientious
d. overseer : wealthy
e. moderator : vicious

289. DEPENDABLE : CAPRICIOUS
a. fallible : cantankerous
b. erasable : obtuse
c. malleable : limpid
d. capable : inept
e. incorrigible : guilty

290. FROND : PALM
a. quill : porcupine
b. blade : evergreen
c. scale : wallaby
d. tusk : alligator
e. blade : fern

291. METAPHOR : SYMBOL
a. pentameter : poem
b. rhythm : melody
c. nuance : song
d. slang : usage
e. analogy : comparison

292. DIRGE : FUNERAL
a. chain : letter
b. bell : church
c. telephone : call
d. jingle : commercial
e. hymn : concerto

293. FERAL : TAME
a. rancid : rational
b. repetitive : recurrent
c. nettlesome : annoying
d. repentant : honorable
e. ephemeral : immortal

294. SPY : CLANDESTINE
a. accountant : meticulous
b. furrier : rambunctious
c. lawyer : ironic
d. shepherd : garrulous
e. astronaut : opulent

295. DOMINANCE : HEGEMONY
a. romance : sympathy
b. furtherance : melancholy
c. independence : autonomy
d. tolerance : philanthropy
e. recompense : hilarity

296. AERIE : EAGLE
a. capital : government
b. bridge : architect
c. unit : apartment
d. kennel : veterinarian
e. house : person

SET 18 (Answers begin on page 138.)

Now try some reasoning questions that ask you to translate English words into an artificial language. First, you will be given a list of three "nonsense" words and their English word meanings. The question or questions that follow will ask you to reverse the process and translate an English word into the artificial language.

Your best approach to this type of question is to look for elements (parts) of the "nonsense" words that repeat. This is the best way to translate from the imaginary language to English. For example, if you know that *linsmerk* means oak tree and *linsdennel* means oak table, then you know that *lins* means oak. And, if *lins* means oak, *merk* must mean tree, and *dennel* must mean table. When you discover what a word element means in English, write it down. Then look for the word elements that appear both on the list and in the answer choices.

297. Here are some words translated from an artificial language.

> *melebroon* means leather shoe
> *blencbroon* means white shoe
> *broonkaal* means shoelaces

Which word could mean "white laces"?
a. blenckaal
b. meleshur
c. melekaal
d. broonblenc

298. Here are some words translated from an artificial language.

> *lilomarj* means green paint
> *lernobix* means vegetable soup
> *bixelam* means soup spoon

Which word could mean "green vegetable"?
a. lilobix
b. lilolerno
c. lernomarj
d. marjlerno

299. Here are some words translated from an artificial language.

> *yoologarn* means red dress
> *glinknara* means wagon wheel
> *yoologlink* means red wagon

Which word could mean "wheelbarrow"?
a. glinkzwet
b. narayoola
c. yoolobrell
d. narapluh

300. Here are some words translated from an artificial language.

> *jabberlota* means pronouncement
> *ennajabber* means mispronounce
> *ennahavre* means misrepresent

Which word could mean "appointment"?
a. relmlota
b. relmjabber
c. havrelota
d. jabbermool

301. Here are some words translated from an artificial language.

> *dionot* means oak tree
> *blyonot* means oak leaf
> *blycrin* means maple leaf

Which word could mean "maple syrup"?
a. blymuth
b. hupponot
c. patricrin
d. crinweel

302. Here are some words translated from an artificial language.

> *agnoscrenia* means poisonous spider
> *delanocrenia* means poisonous snake
> *agnosdeery* means brown spider

Which word could mean "black widow spider"?
a. deeryclostagnos
b. agnosdelano
c. agnosvitriblunin
d. trymuttiagnos

303. Here are some words translated from an artificial language.

> *myncabel* means saddle horse
> *conowir* means trail ride
> *cabelalma* means horse blanket

Which word could mean "horse ride"?
a. cabelwir
b. conocabel
c. almamyn
d. conoalma

304. Here are some words translated from an artificial language.

> *godabim* means kidney stones
> *romzbim* means kidney beans
> *romzbako* means wax beans

Which word could mean "wax statue"?
a. godaromz
b. lazbim
c. wasibako
d. romzpeo

305. Here are some words translated from an artificial language.

> *tamceno* means sky blue
> *cenorax* means blue cheese
> *aplmitl* means star bright

Which word could mean "bright sky"?
a. cenotam
b. mitltam
c. raxmitl
d. aplceno

306. Here are some words translated from an artificial language.

> *gorblflur* means fan belt
> *pixngorbl* means ceiling fan
> *arthtusl* means tile roof

Which word could mean "ceiling tile"?
a. gorbltusl
b. flurgorbl
c. arthflur
d. pixnarth

307. Here are some words translated from an artificial language.

> *hapllesh* means cloudburst
> *srenchoch* means pinball
> *resbosrench* means ninepin

Which word could mean "cloud nine"?
a. leshsrench
b. ochhapl
c. haploch
d. haplresbo

308. Here are some words translated from an artificial language.

> *migenlasan* means cupboard
> *lasanpoen* means boardwalk
> *cuopdansa* means pullman

Which word could mean "walkway"?
a. poenmigen
b. cuopeisel
c. lasandansa
d. poenforc

SET 19 (Answers begin on page 139.)

Here is yet another set of questions that ask you to translate from an imaginary language into English. Remember that the best way to approach these questions is to translate each word element. When you discover what a word element means in English, write it down. Then look for the word elements that appear both on the list and in the answer choices.

309. Here are some words translated from an artificial language.

> *spasirquot* means doghouse
> *torspasir* means sheepdog
> *torlann* means sheepskin

Which word could mean "housefly"?
a. spasirhunde
b. tormill
c. quothunde
d. lannquot

310. Here are some words translated from an artificial language.

> *faur* means bring
> *faury* means bringing
> *faurend* means has brought

Which word could mean "running"?
a. sujjfaurend
b. sujjy
c. endesujj
d. faurmont

311. Here are some words translated from an artificial language.

> *boseamint* means militant
> *insicboca* means habitual
> *insicamene* means habitable

Which word could mean "habitant"?
a. bocabose
b. insicamint
c. bocamint
d. boseamene

312. Here are some words translated from an artificial language.

> *eraneacal* means shipshape
> *araperane* means relationship
> *eranealon* means shipmate

Which word could mean "checkmate"?
a. basalon
b. eranearap
c. alonacal
d. arapalon

313. Here are some words translated from an artificial language.

> *shillenacen* means timetable
> *acenablot* means tablecloth
> *micaerran* means groundwater

Which word could mean "water table"?
a. abloterran
b. micashillen
c. acenmica
d. erranacen

314. Here are some words translated from an artificial language.

> *jusllagen* means obstacle course
> *lagennamer* means coursework
> *ostofifer* means college life

Which word could mean "hard work"?
a. juslnamer
b. remonamer
c. fiferjusl
d. ostonamer

315. Here are some words translated from an artificial language.

> *hamomone* means last minute
> *hamomoze* means last word
> *halligun* means goodness

Which word could mean "wordiness"?
a. mozegun
b. hallimoze
c. monemoze
d. mozehalli

316. Here are some words translated from an artificial language.

> *affongoml* means straw hat
> *affonnagl* means strawberry
> *aftonnagl* means raspberry

Which word could mean "hatband"?
a. naglaffon
b. gomlafton
c. affonnagl
d. gomlnoder

317. Here are some words translated from an artificial language.

> *geromea* means false pretense
> *geneomo* means clock radio
> *gimgene* means alarm clock

Which word could mean "false alarm"?
a. gerogim
b. genegere
c. geromo
d. geneoma

318. Here are some words translated from an artificial language.

> *astaose* means stuffed chair
> *estaose* means leather chair
> *costafut* means liftoff

Which word could mean "chair lift"?
a. futcosta
b. oseesta
c. futose
d. osecosta

319. Here are some words translated from an artificial language.

> *dwilmaga* means powerhouse
> *omaga* means powerful
> *fermaga* means powerless

Which word could mean "overpower"?
a. zenmaga
b. magafer
c. magazen
d. dwilfer

320. Here are some words translated from an artificial language.

hagaupl means apple pie

hagaport means apple juice

hoggagrop means grape jelly

Which word could mean "grape juice"?

a. hoggaport

b. hagaaupl

c. gropport

d. hoggagrop

SET 20 (Answers begin on page 140.)

The questions in this set ask you to match definitions to particular situations. For each question, you will be given a definition and four possible answer choices. Read each definition and all four choices carefully, and find the answer that provides the best example of the given definition. Answer each question *solely* on the basis of the definition given.

321. **Burglary of a Vehicle** occurs when a person breaks into a vehicle without the owner's permission with the intention of stealing something inside. Which situation below is the best example of a Burglary of a Vehicle?
   a. Sam's neighbor has locked his keys inside his car. His arm is injured so he asks Sam to break the vent window on the driver's side and get the car keys out of the ignition.
   b. Jim throws a rock through the passenger window of a parked car, reaches inside, and takes the purse sitting on the passenger seat.
   c. Jeri picks up a rock, throws it through the windshield of a parked car, and runs from the scene.
   d. Anna walks by a parked car and reaches in the open window to pet a dog.

322. It is a crime to harm or threaten to harm someone who has reported a crime or someone who has plans to testify in court about a crime. This is called **Retaliation.** Which situation below is the best example of Retaliation?
   a. Ernie breaks Harold's nose with his fist. Ernie tells Harold he will break both of his legs if he reports him to the police.
   b. Sally tells Larry a secret, and then says she is going to hit him if he tells the secret to Jeff.
   c. Sue is called to be a witness in a robbery trial. The man she is to testify against bumps her shoulder in the crowded hallway in the courthouse and walks on, unaware of what he has done.
   d. A robbery suspect tells his cellmate he wishes he could keep a witness from testifying against him in court.

323. **Trespassing** occurs when a person enters a building without permission from the owner and (1) posted signs or verbal warnings prohibit the presence of unauthorized persons, or (2) the owner or other authorized person asks that person to leave. Which situation below is the best example of Trespassing?

a. Alonzo is hosting a party with his roommate, Manny, who gets angry and tells Alonzo to leave or he'll have him arrested for trespassing.

b. Ben is walking home from school one afternoon, takes a shortcut through Mrs. Benson's front yard, and then hears her yelling at him that she is going to have him arrested for trespassing.

c. Frank is looking at new cars at a dealership after hours when a security guard tells him to leave, which he does immediately.

d. A transient is sleeping in a vacant office building. Posted on the wall is a sign that reads "No Trespassing. Private Property."

324. **Panhandling** occurs when a person asks a stranger for money while on city property. City property includes public streets, sidewalks, or city-owned facilities. Which situation below is the best example of Panhandling?

a. A man approaches Jason on the sidewalk and asks him if he has a quarter in exchange for five nickels.

b. A Salvation Army volunteer on a downtown sidewalk is ringing a hand bell, and a woman tosses some coins into his black kettle as she walks by.

c. Brett is standing at the crosswalk waiting for the streetlight to change, and a man asks her if she wants to buy a raffle ticket.

d. Emilio is standing in the street downtown unlocking his car door when a man walks up to him and asks him for a dollar.

325. **Criminal Mischief** occurs when a person intentionally or knowingly causes damage to or destroys another person's property without the owner's permission. Which situation below is the best example of Criminal Mischief?

a. As Alec is helping Alice move into a new apartment, he drops her $500 lamp and shatters it.

b. When Barry's car runs out of gas on the highway, he steps out of the vehicle and begins smashing out the windows.

c. When Fred sees Angela's new boyfriend's car in her driveway, he walks up to the car, kicks a dent in the fender, and walks on.

d. When Alistair sits down in a chair in a restaurant, the chair breaks underneath him.

326. False Report to a Peace Officer occurs when a person gives a false statement to a peace officer who is conducting a criminal investigation and that person knows his or her statement is a key part of the investigation. Which situation below is the best example of a False Report to a Peace Officer?

a. A resident from a nearby mental hospital calls police to report seeing space aliens stealing dogs from the pet store next door.

b. Ed calls the police to report his stolen car, and police investigators discover that Ed paid friends to steal the car.

c. Betty, a witness to a homicide, tells the investigating officer that the suspect had on a blue shirt, and investigators later find out the shirt was dark green.

d. Janice reports to police that her television has been stolen and then finds out later that a friend came over and borrowed her television without telling her.

327. Driving While Intoxicated occurs when a person is intoxicated while driving or operating a motor vehicle in a public place. Which situation below is the best example of Driving While Intoxicated?

a. Jerry is sitting behind the wheel of his car in a parking lot in front of a bar. The engine is not on, and Jerry has both hands on the wheel and is staring straight ahead.

b. Having drunk several beers, Fred is driving his farm truck around in circles in the back pasture of the family farm.

c. Sandra drives her car off of the highway and into a telephone pole after drinking shots of tequila for four hours at Pete's Corner Bar.

d. Officer Marques pulls a man over for weaving in traffic and discovers the driver was falling asleep at the wheel.

328. **Harassment** occurs when one person, with the intention of annoying, alarming, or tormenting another person, threatens—by telephone or in writing—to harm that person, damage his or her property, or harm a member of his or her family. Which situation below is the best example of Harassment?

a. Lydia leaves a note on Pete's car telling him that she didn't like it when he asked her out on a date and that she'll call police if he ever asks again.

b. Rudy calls Edward on the phone and tells him he is going to break out the headlights on his car if he doesn't stop parking on the street in front of Rudy's house.

c. Tyler calls Ramon and tells him he will be dating Ramon's ex-wife from now on, even though doing so will upset Ramon.

d. Armando writes a note to Julia telling her that, because she is behind on her rent, she will have to move out of the house he is renting to her or he will change the locks on the door and take her property.

329. Possessing a **Hoax Bomb** is a crime when any device or package is used with the intent of making another person believe it is an explosive device or if it causes alarm or reaction by public safety officials. Which situation below is the best example of a Hoax Bomb?

a. Greg has an eight-inch length of pipe filled with finely ground coffee beans and plugged with wax. He places it in his boss's locker at work and waits for her reaction.

b. Stuart is a postal worker and is picking up mail downtown when he thinks he hears ticking coming from a small box he retrieved from a corner mailbox.

c. Harriet is waiting in line at the airport to pass through the metal detector. Security personnel notice a small, pineapple-shaped metal object that looks like a hand grenade in her purse. It turns out to be a gift-wrapped cigarette lighter.

d. Ian is working on a project in the metal shop at school. The instructor notices that Ian is holding a softball-sized black hunk of material that appears to have a fuse trailing from the opening at the top. Ian tells him he was trying to make an oil lamp.

330. Criminal Simulation occurs when, with intent to defraud or harm another, a person alters an object so that it appears to have more worth than it has because of age, antiquity, rarity, or authorship. Which situation below is the best example of Criminal Simulation?

a. Bess Rossburg sews an American flag from scratch and enters it in a contest using the name Betsy Ross.

b. On Elvis's birthday, Eric dresses up as an Elvis look-alike and sells blue velvet paintings of the singer on a street corner.

c. Edith writes a poem onto a scrap of paper, has the paper stained to appear a few decades old, and then tries to sell it to an antique dealer as an Edna St. Vincent Millay original.

d. Wendell finds an old ship's bell in a navy surplus store and tells his friends he got it from one of the men who helped recover the Titanic a few years ago.

331. Theft by Check occurs when a person issues or passes a check with the intent of depriving the owner of property or service available in exchange for the check (1) knowing he or she does not have an account at the financial institution printed on the check or (2) knowing there is an open account at this institution but there isn't enough money to make payment on the check. Which situation below is the best example of Theft by Check?

a. Xena writes a check to the Posey Patrol for flowers for her mother's birthday. The check bounces. The bank notifies her that it covered the check anyway but that her account will be charged $15 for this service.

b. Perla writes a check at the Gypsy Diner. The Diner calls her two days later and tells her that her bank returned it for insufficient funds. She drives to the diner and gives them cash to cover the check.

c. Jacob closed his account today but has left enough money for the rent check he wrote two days ago in that account to clear the bank.

d. Leo closed out his account at Junction Bank three months ago. He still has checks left from that account, so he uses one to pay for his new stereo.

332. Disrupting a Meeting or Procession occurs when a person, with intent to prevent or disrupt a lawful meeting, procession, or gathering, obstructs or interferes with these events either physically or verbally. Which situation below is the best example of Disrupting a Meeting or Procession?
a. Sara is at a city council meeting and gets upset when the mayor refuses to answer her question. She stalks out of the council chambers with her fist raised.
b. Vinnie is at the same council meeting. He is upset because the mayor won't discuss the noise ordinance, so he begins clanging two cymbals together repeatedly.
c. Craig is at the ribbon-cutting ceremony for the new state capitol building. The governor is about to cut the ribbon when Craig yells out, "Reelect the governor."
d. Simone is at a zoning board meeting and learns that she will not be able to open her business in the location she leased. She tells the board members that she will be suing the city and stalks out of the room.

333. Arson occurs when someone starts a fire or causes an explosion with the intent to destroy or damage any building, vehicle, or habitation. Which situation below is the best example of Arson?
a. Samuel places his paper napkin on top of the candle at the table in a restaurant and jumps when it bursts into flames that spread up the window curtains.
b. Leon turns the kitchen-stove burners on high to heat his soup. A potholder catches on fire and sets his girlfriend's kitchen ablaze.
c. Ginger starts a fire in the fireplace and then leaves to run a quick errand. The curtains catch fire and the house begins to burn.
d. Brent sprinkles lighter fluid over the leather seats in his landlord's Mercedes convertible and then throws a lighted match into the car.

334. Disorderly Conduct occurs when a person fights with another person in a public place. Which situation below is the best example of Disorderly Conduct?
a. Alan walks up to Terrence at the bus stop and shoves him. The two men begin trading punches with their fists.
b. Julio and Petra are crossing the street when he begins yelling at her that he is tired of arguing over money.
c. Federico tells his roommate to wash his own dishes and points at a stack of dishes in the sink. His roommate gets mad, and the two men begin hitting each other.
d. Jeff is getting onto the subway when a man elbows him aside. Jeff elbows the man back and then decides to wait for another train.

SET 21 (Answers begin on page 142.)

This set contains additional "situations," many of them dealing with law enforcement. Each question presents a situation and asks you to make a judgment regarding that particular circumstance. Answer each one *solely* on the basis of the information given.

335. For the past two months stereo shops all over the city have been hit by burglars in the early morning hours. Sergeant Adams tells Officer Bryant that he should carefully watch the stores in his area that specialize in stereo equipment. Which one of the following situations should Officer Bryant investigate?

a. a truck with its motor running backed up to the rear door of the House of Stereos at 2 a.m.

b. an elderly couple window shopping at the House of Stereos at 10 p.m.

c. a delivery van marked "House of Stereos" parked in the rear of the store at 11:30 p.m.

d. two teenaged boys intently examining a stereo system in the window of House of Stereos at midnight

336. Mrs. Oneida called police to report that a man was looking into her bedroom window last night around 9:45 p.m. Officer Williams talks to residents in the area and finds out several people have seen a white male dressed in black walking up and down the street at about 10 p.m. for the past week. Officer Williams decides to patrol the area closely and is in the area by 9:30 p.m. Which situation below should she investigate?

a. two teenagers sitting on the curb smoking cigarettes and talking

b. a man wearing black jogging shorts and dark shoes stretching his legs in the driveway of a house

c. a man dressed in dark jeans and a navy blue turtleneck walking rapidly away from the side of a house

d. a man in dark clothing attaching a water hose to the faucet on the side of a house

337. Officer Yang has noticed an increase in graffiti in his area. Store owners are complaining about the damage and have asked him to keep a closer eye out for this problem. Which situation below should Officer Yang investigate?

a. Two teenagers are leaning against a park wall that is completely covered with graffiti.

b. Four teenagers are leaning against the clean white wall of a neighborhood grocery store. One teenager has a spray paint can hanging out of the rear pocket of his baggy pants.

c. Three teenagers are riding bicycles in a grocery store parking lot late at night.

d. Six teenagers are walking along the sidewalk bouncing a basketball and yelling at passing cars while making gang signs with their hands.

338. Merchants in the South Oaks Shopping Mall are upset by a recent rash of purse snatchings in their parking lot. Officer Crandall is closely patrolling the mall area, including the vacant lot behind the stores. Which situation below would Officer Crandall most likely investigate?
   a. a car horn honking continuously in the mall parking lot
   b. a car in the mall parking lot with four flat tires
   c. a woman's voice raised in anger in the mall parking lot
   d. a man running from the direction of the mall through the vacant lot with a bulky object underneath his sweatshirt

339. The owner of the Sun Times Chevrolet dealership tells Officer Chervenack that someone is stealing running boards and other parts off of the vans he has parked in the south lot sometime after 10:30 p.m. Officer Chervenack decides to patrol the area carefully. Which of the following situations should she investigate?
   a. After midnight a man in his early twenties is walking up and down rows of new pick-ups parked near the edge of the dealership.
   b. After midnight a panel truck pulls out of the vacant lot next to the dealership near where the vans are lined up.
   c. After midnight two youths in baggy pants and t-shirts are rollerblading in and out of the new cars on the Sun Times lot.
   d. After midnight a station wagon drives into the lot and stops near the door to the main show room. A man gets out and starts unloading a mop, a bucket, and a broom.

340. Winslow Elementary School is having a criminal mischief problem. Windows are being broken out at the school between 7 p.m. and 6 a.m. Officer Link has talked to the school principal and is keeping a closer eye on the school. Which of the following situations should he investigate?
   a. At 1 a.m. Officer Link watches a man carrying a grocery sack cut through the school-yard and come out on the other side of the school grounds. The officer can see a loaf of bread protruding out of the sack.
   b. At 11 p.m. a car pulls up in the school parking lot. Officer Link sees the driver turn on the cabin light and unfold a map.
   c. Around 11:30 p.m. Officer Link passes the school and sees two figures come out from behind one of the classroom buildings. They stop when they see him and then start walking, each in a different direction.
   d. At 9 p.m. several teenagers skateboard into the parking lot, set up a small wooden ramp, and practice skateboarding tricks.

341. Officer Troy arrives at the scene of a hit-and-run traffic accident. Mrs. Chen tells him she was waiting for the light to change when a car struck her from behind. The driver backed up and left the scene. She saw his license plate as he left, as did three teenaged witnesses waiting for the school bus. The four license-plate numbers below represent what each witness thinks he or she saw. Which one is most likely the license plate of the hit-and-run vehicle?
   a. JXK 12L
   b. JYK 12L
   c. JXK 12I
   d. JXX I2L

342. Officer Littmar is driving by a mall when he is flagged down by four men at a bus stop. They tell him that they just watched a man jump out of a yellow taxi cab and force a woman at gunpoint to get inside the cab with him. They drove away northbound on Exeter Street. All four witnesses said they saw the number painted on the side of the cab and gave Officer Littmar the numbers, which are listed below. Which of the numbers is most likely to be the true number painted on the side of the taxi?
a. 9266
b. 9336
c. 9268
d. 8266

Answer question 343 solely on the basis of the following information.

When an officer goes to a business to pick up a shoplifter who is already in the custody of private security guards, the officer should take the following steps in the order listed:

1. Check with store security personnel to verify that the circumstances fit the criteria for shoplifting.

2. Have store personnel fill out witness statements and a complaint form for shoplifting.

3. Take a photograph of the evidence, and return the evidence to the store.

4. Search the suspect for weapons or contraband.

5. Place the suspect in the patrol car and seatbelt him or her securely.

6. Transport the suspect directly to jail.

343. Officer O'Brien is dispatched to the Blue Moon Art Gallery to pick up a shoplifter. When she arrives, she talks to Jeffrey, the store security guard, who tells her that he watched a man pick up a five-inch long statue, stuff it in his coat pocket, and walk out the front door of the shop. He chased the man down and brought him back to the store. Jeffrey took her into the back room where he gave her a photograph of the statue for her to turn in as evidence. Officer O'Brien searched the prisoner for weapons and then placed him in the patrol car, seatbelting him in securely. They drove straight to the jail where O'Brien booked the suspect for shoplifting. Officer O'Brien's actions were
a. proper, because the incident was obviously a shoplifting
b. improper, because she did not take the statue itself in as evidence
c. proper, because the security guard watched the man carefully before accusing him of anything
d. improper, because she did not have the guard fill out a witness statement or complaint form

Answer question 344 solely on the basis of the following information.

Police officers follow certain procedures when placing a person under arrest and transporting that person in a patrol car. Officers are expected to:

1. Handcuff the prisoner securely.

2. Search the prisoner carefully for possible weapons and contraband.

3. Check the area where the prisoner will be seated in the patrol car for possible weapons and contraband from a previous arrest.

4. Place the prisoner in the patrol car and place a seatbelt around the individual.

5. Transport the prisoner directly to jail.

6. Check the seat and floorboard area where the prisoner was seated after arrival at the jail for possible contraband or weapons from the prisoner.

344. Officer DeVero watched Joe Jackson buy a small vial of cocaine from a dealer on 9th Street and arrested him for possession of a controlled substance. She placed handcuffs on Jackson, searched him for weapons and contraband, and then placed him in the back seat of her patrol car after checking the seat and floorboard area. She placed a seatbelt around the prisoner and drove toward the jail. On the way, she saw a woman roll through a stop sign and pulled her over. She issued the woman a citation and drove on to the jail where she helped the prisoner out of the back seat and checked the area where he had been seated for weapons or contraband. Under these circumstances, the actions taken by Officer DeVero were

a. improper, because she should have also arrested the dealer

b. proper, because she followed proper procedure in arresting and transporting Jackson to jail

c. improper, because she should have taken Jackson directly to jail without stopping

d. proper, because she was able to efficiently handle two situations: the arrest and the traffic violation

345. Officer Manley is called to the scene of a theft of auto parts at the Lucky Lube Auto Parts. The store manager, Alfonso, tells the officer that while Alfonso was waiting on another customer, a woman came inside the store, picked up a pen-shaped tire gauge, and ran out of the store without paying. He shouted at her to stop, but she kept running. Alfonso says he thinks this is the same woman who has been shoplifting up and down the strip mall for the past two weeks. Alfonso describes the woman as white, 5'2", 105 lbs., with light brown hair touching the tops of her shoulders, dark navy-blue wire-rimmed glasses, and a pale blue dress. Officer Manley looks at four other reports to see if the same woman fits as a suspect in the other four thefts.

Suspect in Theft #1: Female, white, 5'2", 105 lbs., shoulder-length brownish hair, glasses, white sandals, stained pale-colored dress.

Suspect in Theft #2: Female, white, 5'3", 110 lbs., with shoulder-length brown hair and wire-rimmed glasses, wearing a green dress.

Suspect in Theft #3: Female, white, 5'5", 125 lbs., dyed light blond hair, blue dress, bare feet.

Suspect in Theft #4: Female, white, 5'2", 112 lbs., light hair worn slightly below the shoulder, thin-framed metal glasses, light-colored sandals, black dress.

In which of the above thefts should Officer Manley suspect Alfonso's suspect?
a. 2, 3, 4
b. 1, 2, 4
c. 1, 2, 3
d. 1, 3, 4

346. Officers Roberts and Reed are on bicycle patrol in the downtown area. Sergeant McElvey tells them that a white male has been committing robberies along the nearby bike path by stepping out of the bushes and threatening bicyclists with an iron pipe until they give him their bicycles. There have been three separate incidents and the suspect descriptions are from three different victims.

Robbery #1: Suspect is a white male, 20–25 years old, 5'9", 145 pounds, with a shaved head, wearing a skull earring in the left ear, floppy white t-shirt, worn light blue jeans, and black combat boots.

Robbery #2: Suspect is a white male, 25–30 years old, dark brown hair in a military-style crew cut, 6'2", 200 pounds, wearing a white t-shirt with the words "Just Do It" on the back, blue surgical scrub pants, and black combat boots.

Robbery #3: Suspect is a white male, 23 years old, 5'10", skinny build, no hair, wearing a Grateful Dead t-shirt, blue baggy pants, dark shoes, and one earring.

Three days after Sergeant McElvey told the officers about the robberies, Officer Reed arrested a suspect for attempting to take a woman's mountain bike from her on the bicycle path. The description of the suspect is as follows:

Robbery #4: Suspect is a white male, 22 years old, 140 pounds, 5'10", with a shaved head and one pierced ear, wearing a plain white t-shirt two sizes too large for him, faded baggy blue jeans, and scuffed black combat boots.

After comparing the suspect description with those in the first three robberies, Officer Reed should consider the arrested man as a suspect in which of the other robberies?

a. Robbery #1, Robbery #2, and Robbery #3
b. Robbery #1, but not Robbery #2 or Robbery #3
c. Robbery #1 and Robbery #3, but not Robbery #2
d. Robbery #1 and Robbery #2, but not Robbery #3

SET 22 (Answers begin on page 144.)

Here's another type of verbal reasoning question. For each item in this set, you will be given a short, informational paragraph and four answer choices. Look for the statement that *must be* true according to the given information. The best way to approach this problem is to read the answer choices in turn, going back each time to look for that exact information in the short passage.

For Questions 347 through 357, find the statement that *must be* true according to the given information.

347. Erin is twelve years old. For three years, she has been asking her parents for a dog. Her parents have told her that they believe a dog would not be happy in an apartment, but they have given her permission to have a bird. Erin has not yet decided what kind of bird she would like to have.

a. Erin's parents like birds better than they like dogs.

b. Erin does not like birds.

c. Erin and her parents live in an apartment.

d. Erin and her parents would like to move.

348. Last summer, Mike spent two weeks at a summer camp. There, he went hiking, swimming, and canoeing. This summer, Mike looks forward to attending a two-week music camp, where he hopes to sing, dance, and learn to play the guitar.

a. Mike's parents want him to learn to play the guitar.

b. Mike prefers music to outdoor activities.

c. Mike goes to some type of camp every summer.

d. Mike likes to sing and dance.

349. The Pacific yew is an evergreen tree that grows in the Pacific Northwest. The Pacific yew has a fleshy, poisonous fruit. Recently, taxol, a substance found in the bark of the Pacific yew, was discovered to be a promising new anticancer drug.

a. Taxol is poisonous when taken by healthy people.

b. Taxol has cured people from various diseases.

c. People should not eat the fruit of the Pacific yew.

d. The Pacific yew was considered worthless until taxol was discovered.

350. On weekends, Mr. Sanchez spends many hours working in his vegetable and flower gardens. Mrs. Sanchez spends her free time reading and listening to classical music. Both Mr. Sanchez and Mrs. Sanchez like to cook.

a. Mr. Sanchez enjoys planting and growing vegetables.

b. Mr. Sanchez does not like classical music.

c. Mrs. Sanchez cooks the vegetables that Mr. Sanchez grows.

d. Mrs. Sanchez enjoys reading nineteenth-century novels.

351. On January 4, 1998, the city of Mitchelville recorded its lowest temperature since 1896. The temperature in Mitchelville on January 4 was 5 degrees Fahrenheit. Two days earlier, two inches of snow fell on the city, and this, too, was an 102-year-old record.

a. The temperature in Mitchelville has never reached 4 degrees Fahrenheit.

b. Deep snow in Mitchelville is extremely rare.

c. Temperatures were not recorded in Mitchelville prior to 1896.

d. Mitchelville has mild winters and mild summers.

352. When they saw that it was snowing, Sheila and Bob Crandall decided to take the train to visit Sheila's Aunt Janet. Aunt Janet lives 218 miles from Sheila and Bob. The roundtrip train tickets cost $32.50 each. On all their other trips to visit Aunt Janet, Sheila and Bob had driven their car.

a. Aunt Janet persuaded Sheila and Bob to take the train.

b. For Sheila and Bob, taking the train is cheaper than driving the car.

c. Sheila and Bob will have to buy four different train tickets.

d. Based on the weather, Sheila and Bob made a decision to take the train.

353. Seahorse populations have declined everywhere that seahorses are fished. During the past five years, seahorse populations have decreased by 50 percent. Last year, biologists met to discuss what might be done to reverse this trend.

a. Seahorses are likely to become extinct within five years.

b. One way to increase seahorse populations is to ban the fishing of seahorses.

c. Biologists from all over the world are working to save the seahorses.

d. Seahorse fishermen have spoken out against the biologists.

354. Vincent has a paper route. Each morning he delivers 37 newspapers to customers in his neighborhood. It takes Vincent 50 minutes to deliver all the papers. If Vincent is sick or has other plans, his friend Thomas, who lives on the same street, will sometimes deliver the papers for him.

a. Vincent and Thomas live in the same neighborhood.

b. It takes Thomas more than 50 minutes to deliver the papers.

c. It is dark outside when Vincent begins his deliveries.

d. Thomas would like to have his own paper route.

355. Georgia is older than her cousin Marsha. Marsha's brother Bart is older than Georgia. When Marsha and Bart are visiting with Georgia, all three like to play a game of Monopoly. Marsha wins more often than Georgia does.

a. When he plays Monopoly with Marsha and Georgia, Bart often loses.

b. Of the three, Georgia is the oldest.

c. Georgia hates to lose at Monopoly.

d. Of the three, Marsha is the youngest.

356. Ten new television shows appeared during the month of September. Five of the shows were sitcoms, three were hour-long dramas, and two were news-magazine shows. By January, only seven of these new shows were still on the air. Five of the shows that remained were sitcoms.

a. Only one of the news-magazine shows remained on the air.

b. Only one of the hour-long dramas remained on the air.

c. At least one of the shows that was cancelled was an hour-long drama.

d. Television viewers prefer sitcoms over hour-long dramas.

357. Sara lives in a large city on the East Coast. Her younger cousin Marlee lives in the Midwest in a small town with fewer than 1,000 residents. Marlee has visited Sara several times during the past five years. In the same period of time Sara has visited Marlee only once.

a. Marlee likes Sara better than Sara likes Marlee.

b. Sara thinks small towns are boring.

c. Sara is older than Marlee.

d. Marlee wants to move to the East Coast.

SET 23 (Answers begin on page 145.)

The next three sets contain short logic problems. Each "problem" consists of three statements. Based on the first two statements, the third statement may be true, false, or uncertain.

Logic problems may appear daunting at first. However, solving these problems can be done in the most straightforward way. Simply "translate" the abstract relationships in the questions into real-world relationships, so you can see the facts more clearly. For example, if the problem is comparing the ages of three people, make a chart and list the names of the people and their possible ages according to the information given. Or, create a diagram using symbols to represent phrases like "older than" or "greater than."

358. Randy is taller than Wendell.

Luis is taller than Randy.

Wendell is taller than Luis.

If the first two statements are true, the third statement is
a. true
b. false
c. uncertain

359. During the past year, Zoe read more books than Jane.

Jane read fewer books than Heather.

Heather read more books than Zoe.

If the first two statements are true, the third statement is
a. true
b. false
c. uncertain

360. All of Joshua's white socks are 100-percent cotton.

Joshua's blue socks are not 100-percent cotton.

All of Joshua's socks are either white or blue.

If the first two statements are true, the third statement is
a. true
b. false
c. uncertain

361. Walnuts cost more than peanuts.

Walnuts cost less than pistachios.

Pistachios cost more than both peanuts and walnuts.

If the first two statements are true, the third statement is
a. true
b. false
c. uncertain

362. All of the houses on Reynolds Road have roofs made of shingles.

No shingles are purple.

None of the houses on Reynolds Road have purple roofs.

If the first two statements are true, the third statement is
a. true
b. false
c. uncertain

363. City A has a higher population than City B.

City C has a lower population than City B.

City A has a lower population than City C.

If the first two statements are true, the third statement is
a. true
b. false
c. uncertain

364. Whiskers weighs less than Paws.

Whiskers weighs more than Tabby.

Of the three cats, Tabby weighs the least.

If the first two statements are true, the third statement is
a. true
b. false
c. uncertain

365. All of Harriet's plants are flowering plants.

Some of Harriet's plants are succulents.

All succulents are flowering plants.

If the first two statements are true, the third statement is
a. true
b. false
c. uncertain

366. Rooms at the Cozy Inn cost less than rooms at the Hide-Away Motel.

Rooms at the Hotel Victoria cost more than rooms at the Hide-Away Motel.

Of the three lodging places, the Hotel Victoria costs the most.

If the first two statements are true, the third statement is
a. true
b. false
c. uncertain

367. Girl Scout Troop 101 sold more cookies than Troop 102.

Troop 103 sold fewer cookies than Troop 102.

Troop 101 sold more cookies than Troop 103.

If the first two statements are true, the third statement is
a. true
b. false
c. uncertain

368. Andre jumps higher than Rodney.

James jumps higher than Andre.

Rodney jumps higher than James.

If the first two statements are true, the third statement is
a. true
b. false
c. uncertain

SET 24 (Answers begin on page 146.)

Some of the logic questions in this set ask you to determine the direction of a particular place in relation to other places. For these "problems," instead of making a chart or grid, draw a very simple map and label North, South, East, and West to help you see where the places are located in relation to each other.

369. Oat cereal has more fiber than corn cereal but less fiber than bran cereal.

Corn cereal has more fiber than rice cereal but less fiber than wheat cereal.

Of the three kinds of cereal, rice cereal has the least amount of fiber.

If the first two statements are true, the third statement is
a. true
b. false
c. uncertain

370. On the day the Barton triplets are born, Jenna weighs more than Jason.

Jason weighs less than Jasmine.

Of the three babies, Jasmine weighs the most.

If the first two statements are true, the third statement is
a. true
b. false
c. uncertain

371. The temperature on Monday was lower than on Tuesday.

The temperature on Wednesday was lower than on Tuesday.

The temperature on Monday was higher than on Wednesday.

If the first two statements are true, the third statement is
a. true
b. false
c. uncertain

372. Spot is bigger than King and smaller than Sugar.

Ralph is smaller than Sugar and bigger than Spot.

King is bigger than Ralph.

If the first two statements are true, the third statement is
a. true
b. false
c. uncertain

373. A fruit basket contains more apples than lemons.

There are more lemons in the basket than there are oranges.

The basket contains more apples than oranges.

If the first two statements are true, the third statement is
a. true
b. false
c. uncertain

374. The Shop and Save Grocery is south of Greenwood Pharmacy.

Rebecca's house is northeast of Greenwood Pharmacy.

Rebecca's house is west of the Shop and Save Grocery.

If the first two statements are true, the third statement is
a. true
b. false
c. uncertain

375. Joe is younger than Kathy.

Mark was born after Joe.

Kathy is older than Mark.

If the first two statements are true, the third statement is
a. true
b. false
c. uncertain

376. All spotted Gangles have long tails.

Short-haired Gangles always have short tails.

Long-tailed Gangles never have short hair.

If the first two statements are true, the third statement is
a. true
b. false
c. uncertain

377. Battery X lasts longer than Battery Y.

Battery Y doesn't last as long as Battery Z.

Battery Z lasts longer than Battery X.

If the first two statements are true, the third statement is
a. true
b. false
c. uncertain

378. Martina is sitting in the desk behind Jerome.

Jerome is sitting in the desk behind Bryant.

Bryant is sitting in the desk behind Martina.

If the first two statements are true, the third statement is
a. true
b. false
c. uncertain

379. Middletown is north of Centerville.

Centerville is east of Penfield.

Penfield is northwest of Middletown.

If the first two statements are true, the third statement is
a. true
b. false
c. uncertain

SET 25 (Answers begin on page 147.)

Here's your last set of "true-false-uncertain" problems. Remember, the best way to answer questions like this is usually to draw a quick diagram or take notes.

380. Taking the train across town is quicker than taking the bus.

Taking the bus across town is slower than driving a car.

Taking the train across town is quicker than driving a car.

If the first two statements are true, the third statement is
a. true
b. false
c. uncertain

381. All Lamels are Signots with buttons.

No yellow Signots have buttons.

No Lamels are yellow.

If the first two statements are true, the third statement is
a. true
b. false
c. uncertain

382. The hotel is two blocks east of the drugstore.

The market is one block west of the hotel.

The drugstore is west of the market.

If the first two statements are true, the third statement is
a. true
b. false
c. uncertain

383. Tom puts on his socks before he puts on his shoes.

He puts on his shirt before he puts on his jacket.

Tom puts on his shoes before he puts on his shirt.

If the first two statements are true, the third statement is
a. true
b. false
c. uncertain

384. Three pencils cost the same as two erasers.

Four erasers cost the same as one ruler.

Pencils are more expensive than rulers.

If the first two statements are true, the third statement is
a. true
b. false
c. uncertain

385. A jar of jelly beans contains more red beans than green.

There are more yellow beans than red.

The jar contains fewer yellow jelly beans than green ones.

If the first two statements are true, the third statement is
a. true
b. false
c. uncertain

386. Cloudy days tend to be more windy than sunny days.

Foggy days tend to be less windy than cloudy days.

Sunny days tend to be less windy than foggy days.

If the first two statements are true, the third statement is
a. true
b. false
c. uncertain

387. The bookstore has a better selection of postcards than the newsstand does.

The selection of postcards at the drugstore is better than at the bookstore.

The drugstore has a better selection of postcards than the bookstore or the newsstand.

If the first two statements are true, the third statement is
a. true
b. false
c. uncertain

388. At a parking lot, a sedan is parked to the right of a pickup and to the left of a sport utility vehicle.

A minivan is parked to the left of the pickup.

The minivan is parked between the pickup and the sedan.

If the first two statements are true, the third statement is
a. true
b. false
c. uncertain

389. A toothpick is useful.

Useful things are valuable.

A toothpick is valuable.

If the first two statements are true, the third statement is
a. true
b. false
c. uncertain

SET 26 (Answers begin on page 148.)

The logic "problems" in this set present you with three true statements: Fact 1, Fact 2, and Fact 3. Then, you are given three more statements (labeled I, II, and III), and you must determine which of these, if any, is also a fact. One or two of the statements could be true; all of the statements could be true; or none of the statements could be true. Choose your answer based *solely* on the information given in the first three facts.

390. Fact 1: Jessica has four children.
Fact 2: Two of the children have blue eyes and two of the children have brown eyes.
Fact 3: Half of the children are girls.

If the first three statements are facts, which of the following statements must also be a fact?
 I. At least one girl has blue eyes.
 II. Two of the children are boys.
 III. The boys have brown eyes.
   a. II only
   b. I and III only
   c. II and III only
   d. None of the statements is a known fact.

391. Fact 1: All hats have brims.
Fact 2: There are black hats and blue hats.
Fact 3: Baseball caps are hats.

If the first three statements are facts, which of the following statements must also be a fact?
 I. All caps have brims.
 II. Some baseball caps are blue.
 III. Baseball caps have no brims.
   a. I only
   b. II only
   c. I, II, and III
   d. None of the statements is a known fact.

392. Fact 1: All chickens are birds.
Fact 2: Some chickens are hens.
Fact 3: Female birds lay eggs.

If the first three statements are facts, which of the following statements must also be a fact?
 I. All birds lay eggs.
 II. Hens are birds.
 III. Some chickens are not hens.
   a. II only
   b. II and III only
   c. I, II and III
   d. None of the statements is a known fact.

393. Fact 1: Most stuffed toys are stuffed with beans.

Fact 2: There are stuffed bears and stuffed tigers.

Fact 3: Some chairs are stuffed with beans.

If the first three statements are facts, which of the following statements must also be a fact?

I. Only children's chairs are stuffed with beans.

II. All stuffed tigers are stuffed with beans.

III. Stuffed monkeys are not stuffed with beans.

a. I only

b. II only

c. II and III only

d. None of the statements is a known fact.

394. Fact 1: Pictures can tell a story.

Fact 2: All storybooks have pictures.

Fact 3: Some storybooks have words.

If the first three statements are facts, which of the following statements must also be a fact?

I. Pictures can tell a story better than words can.

II. The stories in storybooks are very simple.

III. Some storybooks have both words and pictures.

a. I only

b. II only

c. III only

d. None of the statements is a known fact.

395. Fact 1: Robert has four vehicles.

Fact 2: Two of the vehicles are red.

Fact 3: One of the vehicles is a minivan.

If the first three statements are facts, which of the following statements must also be a fact?

I. Robert has a red minivan.

II. Robert has three cars.

III. Robert's favorite color is red.

a. I only

b. II only

c. II and III only

d. None of the statements is a known fact.

396. Fact 1: Islands are surrounded by water.
Fact 2: Maui is an island.
Fact 3: Maui was formed by a volcano.

If the first three statements are facts, which of the following statements must also be a fact?
   I. Maui is surrounded by water.
   II. All islands are formed by volcanoes.
   III. All volcanoes are on islands.
      a. I only
      b. III only
      c. I and II only
      d. None of the statements is a known fact.

397. Fact 1: All drink mixes are beverages.
Fact 2: All beverages are drinkable.
Fact 3: Some beverages are red.

If the first three statements are facts, which of the following statements must also be a fact?
   I. Some drink mixes are red.
   II. All beverages are drink mixes.
   III. All red drink mixes are drinkable.
      a. I only
      b. II only
      c. I and III
      d. None of the statements is a known fact.

398. Fact 1: Eyeglass frames cost between $35 and $350.
Fact 2: Some eyeglass frames are made of titanium.
Fact 3: Some eyeglass frames are made of plastic.

If the first three statements are facts, which of the following statements must also be a fact?
   I. Titanium eyeglass frames cost more than plastic frames.
   II. Expensive eyeglass frames last longer than cheap frames.
   III. Only a few eyeglass frames cost less than $35.
      a. II only
      b. I and II only
      c. II and III only
      d. None of the statements is a known fact.

399. Fact 1: Some pens don't write.
Fact 2: All blue pens write.
Fact 3: Some writing utensils are pens.

If the first three statements are facts, which of the following statements must also be a fact?
   I. Some writing utensils don't write.
   II. Some writing utensils are blue.
   III. Some blue writing utensils don't write.
      a. II only
      b. I and II only
      c. II and III only
      d. None of the statements is a known fact.

400. Fact 1: Mary said, "Ann and I both have cats."

Fact 2: Ann said, "I don't have a cat."

Fact 3: Mary always tells the truth, but Ann sometimes lies.

If the first three statements are facts, which of the following statements must also be a fact?

I. Ann has a cat.

II. Mary has a cat.

III. Ann is lying.

a. II only

b. I and II only

c. I, II, and III

d. None of the statements is a known fact.

401. Fact 1: All dogs like to run.

Fact 2: Some dogs like to swim.

Fact 3: Some dogs look like their masters.

If the first three statements are facts, which of the following statements must also be a fact?

I. All dogs who like to swim look like their masters.

II. Dogs who like to swim also like to run.

III. Dogs who like to run do not look like their masters.

a. I only

b. II only

c. II and III only

d. None of the statements is a known fact.

SET 27 (Answers begin on page 149.)

Here is yet another set of logic questions. The logic "problems" in this set are somewhat more complex than the ones in the previous sets, but your approach should be the same. Make a chart or grid so that you can order the given information.

402. Police officers are in pursuit of a stolen vehicle. Officer Baker is directly behind the stolen car. Officer Lopez is behind Baker; Officer O'Malley is behind Lopez. Officer Reinhart is ahead of the stolen car and coming from the opposite direction. Officer Reinhart makes a U-turn and joins the pursuit. He pulls in behind Officer Lopez. Officer Baker pulls up on the driver's side of the stolen vehicle and Officer Lopez pulls up on the other side. Which officer is directly behind the vehicle?

 a. Baker

 b. Lopez

 c. O'Malley

 d. Reinhart

403. Nurse Kemp has worked more night shifts in a row than Nurse Rogers, who has worked five. Nurse Miller has worked fifteen night shifts in a row, more than Nurses Kemp and Rogers combined. Nurse Calvin has worked eight night shifts in a row, less than Nurse Kemp. How many night shifts in a row has Nurse Kemp worked?

 a. eight

 b. nine

 c. ten

 d. eleven

404. Four friends in the sixth grade were sharing a pizza. They decided that the oldest friend would get the extra piece. Randy is two months older than Greg, who is three months younger than Ned. Kent is one month older than Greg. Who should get the extra piece of pizza?

 a. Randy

 b. Greg

 c. Ned

 d. Kent

405. The police are staking out a suspected crack house. Officer Michaels is in front of the house. Officer Roth is in the alley behind the house. Officer Jensen is covering the windows on the north side, Officer Sheen those on the south. If Officer Michaels switches places with Officer Jensen, and Jensen then switches places with Officer Sheen, where is Officer Sheen?

 a. in the alley behind the house

 b. on the north side of the house

 c. in front of the house

 d. on the south side of the house

406. In a four-day period—Monday through Thursday—each of the following temporary office workers worked only one day, each a different day. Ms. Johnson was scheduled to work on Monday, but she traded with Mr. Carter, who was originally scheduled to work on Wednesday. Ms. Falk traded with Mr. Kirk, who was originally scheduled to work on Thursday. After all the switching was done, who worked on Tuesday?

 a. Mr. Carter

 b. Ms. Falk

 c. Ms. Johnson

 d. Mr. Kirk

407. The high school math department needs to appoint a new chairperson, which will be based on seniority. Ms. West has less seniority than Mr. Temple, but more than Ms. Brody. Mr. Rhodes has more seniority than Ms. West, but less than Mr. Temple. Mr. Temple doesn't want the job. Who will be the new math department chairperson?

a. Mr. Rhodes
b. Mr. Temple
c. Ms. West
d. Ms. Brody

408. Four people witnessed a mugging. Each gave a different description of the mugger. Which description is probably right?

a. He was average height, thin, and middle-aged.
b. He was tall, thin, and middle-aged.
c. He was tall, thin, and young.
d. He was tall, of average weight, and middle-aged.

409. Due to jail overcrowding, one prisoner must be moved from the city jail to the county jail. The officers have been instructed to move the prisoner who is charged with committing the most severe offense and who has the longest record. Robb has been arrested this time for a misdemeanor and has been arrested seven times before. James has been arrested for a felony and has been arrested fewer times than Robb. Bush has been arrested for a more serious crime than James and has been arrested more times than Robb. Michaels has been arrested for a misdemeanor, and it is his third offense. Who will be moved to the county jail?

a. Robb
b. Bush
c. Michaels
d. James

410. Four defensive football players are chasing the opposing wide receiver, who has the ball. Calvin is directly behind the ball carrier. Jenkins and Burton are side by side behind Calvin. Zeller is behind Jenkins and Burton. Calvin tries for the tackle but misses and falls. Burton trips. A defensive player tackles the receiver. Which one?

a. Burton
b. Zeller
c. Jenkins
d. Calvin

411. The alarm goes off at the State National Bank. Officer Manson is patrolling in his squad car ten miles away. Officer Fromme is patrolling five miles away, Officer Smith, seven miles. Officer Sexton is farther away than Fromme, but closer than Smith. Approximately how far away from the bank is Sexton?
a. nine miles
b. seven miles
c. eight miles
d. six miles

412. Ms. Forest likes to let her students choose who their partners will be; however, no pair of students may work together more than seven class periods in a row. Adam and Baxter have studied together seven class periods in a row. Carter and Dennis have worked together three class periods in a row. Carter does not want to work with Adam. Who should be assigned to work with Baxter?
a. Carter
b. Adam
c. Dennis
d. Forest

413. At the baseball game, Henry was sitting in seat 253. Marla was sitting to the right of Henry in seat 254. In the seat to the left of Henry was George. Inez was sitting to the left of George. Which seat is Inez sitting in?
a. 251
b. 254
c. 255
d. 256

SET 28 (Answers begin on page 150.)

Questions that involve analytical reasoning—better known as "logic games"—tend to inspire fear in most test takers. These games give the most trouble to test takers who haven't defined a specific method for solving these problems. The best way to attack "logic games" is to have a plan. When solving the problems in this set, try the following strategy:

1. Know the rules of the logic game and what each rule means.

2. Draw up an easy-to-reference diagram that includes all of the game's information.

3. Look for common elements in the rules; you can combine these to make deductions.

4. Read the questions carefully; be sure you know what is being asked before you try to answer the question.

Now, try solving the "logic games" in this set.

Answer questions 414 through 416 on the basis of the information below.

The government of an island nation is in the process of deciding how to spend its limited income. It has $7 million left in its budget and eight programs to choose among. There is no provision in the constitution to have a surplus, and each program has requested the minimum amount they need; in other words, no program may be partially funded. The programs and their funding requests are:

- Hurricane preparedness: $2.5 million
- Harbor improvements: $1 million
- School music program: $0.5 million
- Senate office building remodeling: $1.5 million
- Agricultural subsidy program: $2 million
- National radio: $0.5 million
- Small business loan program: $3 million
- International airport: $4 million

414. If the legislature decides to fund the agricultural subsidy program, national radio, and the small business loan program, the only other single program that can be funded is
   a. hurricane preparedness
   b. harbor improvements
   c. school music program
   d. senate office building remodeling
   e. international airport

LearningExpress Skill Builders Practice   81

415. If the legislature decides to fund the agricultural subsidy program, national radio, and the small business loan program, what two other programs could they fund?
a. harbor improvements and international airport
b. harbor improvements and school music program
c. hurricane preparedness and school music program
d. hurricane preparedness and international airport
e. harbor improvements and hurricane preparedness

416. Senators from urban areas are very concerned about assuring that there will be funding for a new international airport. Senators from rural areas refuse to fund anything until money for agricultural subsidies is appropriated. If the legislature funds these two programs, on which of the following could they spend the rest of the money?
a. the school music program and national radio
b. hurricane preparedness
c. harbor improvements and the school music program
d. small business loan program
e. national radio and senate office building remodeling

Answer questions 417 through 418 on the basis of the information below.

A weekly television show routinely stars six actors, J, K, L, M, N, and O. Since the show has been on the air for a long time, some of the actors are good friends and some do not get along at all. In an effort to keep peace, the director sees to it that friends work together and enemies do not. Also, as the actors have become more popular, some of them need time off to do other projects. In order to keep the schedule working, the director has a few things she must be aware of:

- J will only work on episodes on which M is working.
- N will not work with K under any circumstances.
- M can only work every other week, in order to be free to film a movie
- At least three of the actors must appear in every weekly episode.

417. In a show about L getting a job at the same company J already works for and K used to work for, all three actors will appear. Which of the following is true about the other actors who may appear?
a. M, N, and O must all appear.
b. M may appear and N must appear.
c. M must appear and O may appear.
d. O may appear and N may appear.
e. Only O may appear.

418. The next week, the show involves N's new car and O's new refrigerator. Which of the following is true about the other actors who may appear?
a. M, J, L, and K all may appear.
b. J, L, and K must appear.
c. Only K may appear.
d. Only L may appear.
e. L and K must appear.

Answer questions 419 through 421 on the basis of the information below.

A cinema complex with six movie theaters never shows the same movie in more than one theater. None of the theaters is the same size as any other, with number 1 being the largest and going in order to number 6, the smallest. The theater also has the following rules:

- It will never show more than two R-rated movies at once.
- It will always show at least one G-rated movie and one PG-rated movie in the two middle-sized theaters (theaters 3 and 4).
- It will never show more than one foreign film at a time and never in the biggest theater.
- The starting times of movies will be staggered by fifteen minutes and will always be on the quarter hour.
- Employees need twenty minutes between showings to clean the theaters.

The cinema has the following films to choose from this particular week:

Shout, rated R
Que Pasa, a Spanish film rated PG
Abra Cadabra, rated G
Lessons, rated R
Jealousy, rated PG
Mist, a Swedish film rated R
Trek, rated NC-17
Fly, rated G

419. Which one of the following is an acceptable listing of films to show this week?
a. *Shout, Mist, Trek, Que Pasa, Fly,* and *Jealousy*
b. *Shout, Mist, Trek, Fly, Jealousy,* and *Abra Cadabra*
c. *Que Pasa, Lessons, Mist, Shout, Abra Cadabra,* and *Trek*
d. *Shout, Lessons, Mist, Trek, Fly,* and *Jealousy*
e. *Shout, Fly, Trek, Lessons, Abra Cadabra,* and *Mist*

420. If *Shout* starts at 8:30, *Mist* at 8:15, *Trek* at 8:00, *Fly* at 7:45, *Jealousy* at 7:30, and *Abra Cadabra* at 7:15, and each movie is exactly 2 hours long, at what time will the next showing of *Trek* start?
a. 10:00
b. 10:15
c. 10:30
d. 10:45
e. 11:00

421. The movies this week are showing in the following theaters:

Theater 1: *Shout*

Theater 2: *Trek*

Theater 3: *Abra Cadabra*

Theater 4: *Jealousy*

Theater 5: *Fly*

Theater 6: *Mist*

Shout is doing the most business, followed by *Trek* and, to the management's surprise, *Mist*. The management wants to move *Mist* to a larger theater. Which theater is the most logical?

a. Theater 1
b. Theater 2
c. Theater 3
d. Theater 4
e. Theater 5

Answer questions 422 through 423 on the basis of the information below.

The six top songs (not in order) of 1968 were:

"People Got to Be Free" by The Rascals
"Sittin' on the Dock of the Bay" by Otis Redding
"Honey" by Bobby Goldsboro
"Sunshine of Your Love" by Cream
"Love Is Blue" by Paul Mauriat & His Orchestra
"Hey Jude" by The Beatles

Here are some rules about the order of the songs:

- The Beatles and Cream do not appear next to each other on the list.
- The number-one song is not "Love Is Blue."
- The songs by individual artists are numbers 3 and 4.
- The Rascals appear right before Cream and right after Otis Redding.

422. Which of the following is true?

a. Song #3 is "Honey" by Bobby Goldsboro
b. Song #6 is "Hey Jude" by the Beatles
c. Song #1 is "Sittin' on the Dock of the Bay" by Otis Redding
d. Song #1 is "Sunshine of Your Love" by Cream
e. Song #3 is "Sittin' on the Dock of the Bay" by Otis Redding

423. Which of the following is the correct order of songs?

    a. "Honey," "Love is Blue," "People Got To Be Free," "Sunshine of Your Love," "Sittin' on the Dock of the Bay," "Hey Jude"

    b. "Love is Blue," "Hey Jude," "Honey," "Sittin' on the Dock of the Bay," "People Got to be Free," "Sunshine of Your Love"

    c. "Sunshine of Your Love," "People Got to Be Free," "Sittin' on the Dock of the Bay," "Honey," "Love is Blue," "Hey Jude"

    d. "Hey Jude," "Love is Blue," "Honey," "Sittin' on the Dock of the Bay," "People Got to be Free," "Sunshine of Your Love"

    e. "Honey," "Sittin' on the Dock of the Bay," "Hey Jude," "Sunshine of Your Love," "People Got to be Free," "Love is Blue"

SET 29 (Answers begin on page 151.)

If you're having trouble after the first set of logic games, there's a bonus for you—a complete explanation of questions 424 and 425 in the answers section, with a step-by-step explanation of how to set up a table to answer the questions.

Answer questions 424 and 425 on the basis of the information below.

At a Halloween party where people were asked to dress as an object that represented their professions, Quentin, Rachel, Sarah, Thomas, and Ulysses were among the guests. The costumes included a flower, a pencil, a spoon, a camera, and a thermometer. The professions included a photographer, a florist, a doctor, an accountant, and a chef.

- Quentin is an accountant.
- Neither Rachel nor Sarah was dressed as a spoon.
- None of the men is a doctor.
- Thomas is dressed as a camera.
- Sarah is a florist.

424. Which person is dressed as a thermometer?
- a. Quentin
- b. Rachel
- c. Sarah
- d. Thomas
- e. Ulysses

425. What is Ulysses's profession?
- a. photographer
- b. florist
- c. doctor
- d. accountant
- e. chef

Answer questions 426 through 428 on the basis of the information below.

Evan is a waiter in a café. After he turns in orders for the six people sitting at the counter—each of whom is eating alone and is sitting in chairs numbered 1 through 6—the cook opens a window in the kitchen and the order slips get messed up. Here's what Evan remembers about the orders:

- The entree orders are: fried eggs, a hamburger, a cheeseburger, a vegetable burger, soup, and a ham sandwich.
- The two people who did not order sandwiches are sitting at spaces 3 and 4.
- The person who ordered the cheeseburger and the one who ordered the hamburger are not sitting next to each other.
- The person in space number 5 is a regular. She will not sit next to anyone who is eating ham.
- The person eating the vegetable burger is not sitting in space 2, but is sitting between the person who ordered fried eggs and the one who ordered a cheeseburger.
- The customer who ordered the hamburger is not sitting next to the customer who ordered soup.

426. To which customer should Evan serve the vegetable burger?
- a. the customer in chair 2
- b. the customer in chair 3
- c. the customer in chair 4
- d. the customer in chair 5
- e. the customer in chair 6

427. To which customer should Evan serve the soup?
a. the customer in chair 1
b. the customer in chair 2
c. the customer in chair 3
d. the customer in chair 4
e. the customer in chair 5

428. To which customer should Evan serve the ham sandwich?
a. the customer in chair 1
b. the customer in chair 2
c. the customer in chair 4
d. the customer in chair 5
e. the customer in chair 6

Use the additional information below, along with the information before question 426, to answer questions 429 and 430.

Now Evan has to decide who gets which side dish. Here is what he remembers, in addition to the above information, about the orders, which were: cole slaw, hash browns, onion rings, potato salad, french fries, and lettuce salad.

- The person who ordered soup did not order french fries, hash browns, onion rings, or a lettuce salad.
- The person who ordered onion rings is sitting in chair 6
- The person who ordered potato salad is sitting between the person who ordered cole slaw and the one who ordered hash browns.
- The person who ordered a vegetable burger ordered a lettuce salad.
- The hash browns were ordered by the customer who ordered fried eggs.

429. With which entrée does the potato salad belong?
a. soup
b. hamburger
c. cheeseburger
d. fried eggs
e. ham sandwich

430. With which entrée do the french fries belong?
a. soup
b. cheeseburger
c. hamburger
d. fried eggs
e. ham sandwich

Answer questions 431 through 433 on the basis of the information below.

At a small company, parking spaces are reserved for the top executives: CEO, President, Vice President, Secretary, and Treasurer—with the spaces lined up in that order. The parking lot guard can tell at a glance if the cars are parked correctly by looking at the color of the cars. The cars are yellow, green, purple, red, and blue, and the executives' names are Alice, Bert, Cheryl, David, and Enid.

- The car in the first space is red.
- A blue car is parked between the red car and the green car.
- The car in the last space is purple.
- The secretary drives a yellow car.
- Alice's car is parked next to David's.
- Enid drives a green car.
- Bert's car is parked between Cheryl's and Enid's.
- David's car is parked in the last space.

431. What color is the vice-president's car?
   a. green
   b. yellow
   c. blue
   d. purple
   e. red

432. Who is the CEO?
   a. Alice
   b. Bert
   c. Cheryl
   d. David
   e. Enid

433. Who is the secretary?
   a. Enid
   b. David
   c. Cheryl
   d. Bert
   e. Alice

SET 30 (Answers begin on page 153.)

Remember, the best way to answer these logic game questions is to attack the information systematically. Make a diagram outlining all the given information. There's always at least one fact that can serve as your starting point, the place to begin eliminating possibilities.

Answer questions 434 through 436 on the basis of the information below.

Five towns—Fulton, Groton, Hudson, Ivy, and Jersey—which are covered by the same newspaper, all have excellent soccer teams. The teams are named the Panthers, the Whippets, the Antelopes, the Kangaroos, and the Gazelles. The sports reporter, who has just started at the newspaper, has to be careful not to get them confused. Here is what she knows:

- The team in Fulton has beaten the Antelopes, Panthers, and Kangaroos.
- The Whippets have beaten the teams in Jersey, Hudson, and Fulton.
- The Antelopes are in Groton.
- The team in Hudson is not the Kangaroos.

434. Where are the Whippets?
   a. Fulton
   b. Groton
   c. Hudson
   d. Ivy
   e. Jersey

435. Where are the Panthers?
   a. Ivy
   b. Jersey
   c. Fulton
   d. Groton
   e. Hudson

436. What team is in Fulton?
   a. Panthers
   b. Gazelles
   c. Whippets
   d. Kangaroos
   e. Antelopes

Answer questions 437 through 439 on the basis of the information below.

Henri delivers flowers for a local florist. One lovely day, he left the windows open on the delivery van and the cards all blew off the bouquets. He has to figure out who gets which flowers. He has five bouquets, each of which has only one kind of flower: daisies, roses, carnations, iris, and gladioli. He has five cards with names on them: a birthday card for Inez, a congratulations-on-your-promotion card for Jenny, a graduation card for Kevin, an anniversary card for Liz, and a housewarming card for Michael. Here's what Henri knows:

- Roses are Jenny's favorite flower and what her friends always send.
- Gladioli are traditionally sent for a housewarming.
- Kevin is allergic to daisies and iris.
- Liz is allergic to daisies and roses.
- Neither Liz nor Inez has moved recently.

437. Which flowers should be delivered to Kevin?
   a. carnations
   b. iris
   c. gladioli
   d. daisies
   e. roses

438. Who should get the housewarming gladioli?
   a. Jenny
   b. Kevin
   c. Liz
   d. Michael
   e. Inez

439. Which flowers should be delivered to Liz?
   a. gladioli
   b. daisies
   c. roses
   d. carnations
   e. iris

Answer questions 440 through 443 on the basis of the information below.

Five cities all got more rain than usual this year. The five cities are: Last Stand, Mile City, New Town, Olliopolis, and Polberg. The cities are located in five different areas of the country: the mountains, the forest, the coast, the desert, and in a valley. The rainfall amounts were: 12 inches, 27 inches, 32 inches, 44 inches, and 65 inches.

- The city in the desert got the least rain; the city in the forest got the most rain.
- New Town is in the mountains.
- Last Stand got more rain than Olliopolis.
- Mile City got more rain than Polberg, but less rain than New Town.
- Olliopolis got 44 inches of rain.
- The city in the mountains got 32 inches of rain; the city on the coast got 27 inches of rain.

440. Which city is in the desert?
   a. Last Stand
   b. Mile City
   c. New Town
   d. Olliopolis
   e. Polberg

441. Which city got the most rain?
   a. Last Stand
   b. Mile City
   c. New Town
   d. Olliopolis
   e. Polberg

442. How much rain did Mile City get?
   a. 12 inches
   b. 27 inches
   c. 32 inches
   d. 44 inches
   e. 65 inches

443. Where is Olliopolis located?
   a. the mountains
   b. the coast
   c. in a valley
   d. the desert
   e. the forest

SET 31 (Answers begin on page 154.)

Here's one more set of "logic games." Remember, mapping out the game using all the given information is the most efficient way to attack this type of question.

Answer questions 444 through 447 on the basis of the information below.

Eleanor is in charge of seating the speakers at a table. In addition to the moderator, there will be a pilot, a writer, an attorney, and an explorer. The speakers' names are Gary, Heloise, Jarrod, Kate, and Lane.

- The moderator must sit in the middle, in seat #3.
- The attorney cannot sit next to the explorer.
- Lane is the pilot.
- The writer and the attorney sit on either side of the moderator.
- Heloise, who is not the moderator, sits between Kate and Jarrod.
- The moderator does not sit next to Jarrod or Lane.
- Gary, who is the attorney, sits in seat #4.

444. Who is the moderator?
- a. Lane
- b. Gary
- c. Heloise
- d. Kate
- e. Jarrod

445. Where does Jarrod sit?
- a. seat #1
- b. seat #2
- c. seat #3
- d. seat #4
- e. seat #5

446. What occupation does Jarrod hold?
- a. a moderator
- b. a pilot
- c. a writer
- d. an attorney
- e. an explorer

447. Who is the writer?
- a. Gary
- b. Heloise
- c. Jarrod
- d. Kate
- e. Lane

Answer question 448 on the basis of the information below.

Zinnia has a small container garden on her balcony. Each spring, she only has room to plant three vegetables. Because five vegetables are her favorites, she has worked out a schedule to plant each at least once every two years. The vegetables are: beans, cabbage, carrots, peppers, and tomatoes.

- Tomatoes are her favorites and she plants them every year.
- Each year, she plants only one vegetable that begins with the letter "C."
- She never plants carrots and peppers in the same year.
- She will plant cabbage in the second year.

448. In what order does she plant the vegetables in the next two years?
- a. first year: tomatoes, carrots, cabbage
  second year: tomatoes, peppers, beans
- b. first year: tomatoes, peppers, beans
  second year: cabbage, carrots, tomatoes
- c. first year: tomatoes, carrots, peppers
  second year: tomatoes, cabbage, beans
- d. first year: tomatoes, carrots, beans
  second year: tomatoes, cabbage, peppers
- e. first year: tomatoes, cabbage, peppers
  second year: carrots, cabbage, beans

Answer questions 449 through 453 on the basis of the information below.

Five roommates—Randy, Sally, Terry, Uma, and Vernon—each do one housekeeping task—mopping, sweeping, laundry, vacuuming, or dusting—one day a week, Monday through Friday.

- Vernon does not vacuum and does not do his task on Tuesday.
- Sally does the dusting, and does not do it on Monday or Friday.
- The mopping is done on Thursday.
- Terry does his task, which is not vacuuming, on Wednesday.
- The laundry is done on Friday, and not by Uma.
- Randy does his task on Monday.

449. When does Sally do the dusting?
- a. Friday
- b. Monday
- c. Tuesday
- d. Wednesday
- e. Thursday

450. What task does Terry do on Wednesday?
- a. vacuuming
- b. dusting
- c. mopping
- d. sweeping
- e. laundry

451. What day is the vacuuming done?
- a. Friday
- b. Monday
- c. Tuesday
- d. Wednesday
- e. Thursday

452. What task does Vernon do?

a. vacuuming

b. dusting

c. mopping

d. sweeping

e. laundry

453. What day does Uma do her task?

a. Monday

b. Tuesday

c. Wednesday

d. Thursday

e. Friday

SET 32 (Answers begin on page 155.)

Each of the questions in this set contains a short paragraph, and each paragraph presents an argument. Your task is the read the paragraph carefully and determine the main point the author is trying to make. What conclusion can be drawn from the argument? Each paragraph is followed by five statements. One statement supports the author's argument better than the others do. The best way to approach these questions is first read the paragraph and then restate the author's main argument, or conclusion, in your own words.

454. If you're a fitness walker, there is no need for a commute to a health club. Your neighborhood can be your health club. You don't need a lot of fancy equipment to get a good workout either. All you need is a well-designed pair of athletic shoes.

This paragraph best supports the statement that
a. fitness walking is a better form of exercise than weight lifting.
b. a membership in a health club is a poor investment.
c. walking outdoors provides a better workout than walking indoors.
d. fitness walking is a convenient and valuable form of exercise.
e. poorly designed athletic shoes can cause major foot injuries.

455. It is well-known that the world urgently needs adequate distribution of food, so that everyone gets enough. Adequate distribution of medicine is just as urgent. Medical expertise and medical supplies need to be redistributed throughout the world so that people in emerging nations will have proper medical care.

This paragraph best supports the statement that
a. the majority of the people in the world have never been seen by a doctor.
b. food production in emerging nations has slowed during the past several years.
c. most of the world's doctors are selfish about giving time and money to the poor.
d. the medical-supply industry should step up production of its products.
e. many people who live in emerging nations are not receiving proper medical care.

456. The criminal justice system needs to change. The system could be more just if it allowed victims the opportunity to confront the person who has harmed them. Also, mediation between victims and their offenders would give the offenders a chance to apologize for the harm they have done.

This paragraph best supports the statement that victims of a crime should
a. learn to forgive their offenders.
b. have the right to confront their offenders.
c. learn the art of mediation.
d. insist that their offenders be punished.
e. have the right to impose a sentence on their offenders.

457. In the past, suggesting a gas tax has usually been thought of as political poison. But that doesn't seem to be the case today. Several states are pushing bills in their state legislatures that would cut income or property taxes and make up the revenue with taxes on fossil fuel.

This paragraph best supports the statement that
a. gas taxes produce more revenue than income taxes.
b. states with low income tax rates are increasing their gas taxes.
c. state legislators no longer fear increasing gas taxes.
d. taxes on fossil fuels are more popular than property taxes.
e. all tax increases threaten the jobs of lawmakers.

458. A few states in this country are considering legislation that would prohibit schools from using calculators before the sixth grade. Other states take a different position. Some states are insisting on the purchase of graphing calculators for every student in middle school.

This paragraph best supports the statement that in this country
a. there are at least two opinions about the use of calculators in schools.
b. calculators are frequently a detriment to learning math.
c. state legislators are more involved in education than ever before.
d. the price graphing calculators is less when schools buy in bulk.
e. the argument against calculators in schools is unfounded.

459. One of the warmest winters on record has put consumers in the mood to spend money. Spending is likely to be the strongest in thirteen years. During the month of February, sales of existing single-family homes hit an annual record rate of 4.75 million.

This paragraph best supports the statement that
a. consumer spending will be higher thirteen years from now than it is today.
b. more people buy houses in the month of February than in any other month.
c. during the winter months, the prices of single-family homes are the lowest.
d. there were about 4 million homes for sale during the month of February.
e. warm winter weather is likely to affect the rate of home sales.

460. One New York publisher has estimated that 50,000 to 60,000 people in the United States want an anthology that includes the complete works of William Shakespeare. And what accounts for this renewed interest in Shakespeare? As scholars point out, his psychological insights into both male and female characters are amazing even today.

This paragraph best supports the statement that
a. Shakespeare's characters are more interesting than fictional characters today.
b. people today are interested in Shakespeare's work because of the characters.
c. academic scholars are putting together an anthology of Shakespeare's work.
d. New Yorkers have a renewed interested in the work of Shakespeare.
e. Shakespeare was a psychiatrist as well as a playwright.

461. Today's work force has a new set of social values. Ten years ago, a manager who was offered a promotion in a distant city would not have questioned the move. Today, a manager in that same situation might choose family happiness instead of career advancement.

This paragraph best supports the statement that

a. most managers are not loyal to the corporations for which they work.

b. businesses today do not understand their employees' needs.

c. employees' social values have changed over the past ten years.

d. career advancement is not important to today's business managers.

e. companies should require their employees to accept promotions.

462. Generation Xers are those people born roughly between 1965 and 1981. As employees, Generation Xers tend to be more challenged when they can carry out tasks independently. This makes Generation Xers the most entrepreneurial generation in history.

This paragraph best supports the statement that Generation Xers

a. work harder than people from other generations.

b. have a tendency to be self-directed workers.

c. have an interest in making history.

d. tend to work in jobs that require risk-taking behavior.

e. like to challenge their bosses' work attitudes.

463. In the last presidential election in the U.S., fewer than fifty percent of all eligible voters cast their votes. Rather than bemoan the low level of participation in elections, we should make voting compulsory. If citizens have a duty to vote, as they have a duty to pay their taxes, then there would be a penalty for not voting. Because it is largely the poor who do not vote, the poor would gain more political power.

This paragraph best supports the statement that

a. lower voter participation results in inept leaders.

b. voter participation is declining because there are more poor people in the U.S.

c. citizens should cast their votes at the same time as they pay their taxes.

d. most democracies face the problem of low voter turnout.

e. eligible voters in the U.S. should be required to vote in presidential elections.

SET 33 (Answers begin on page 157.)

For more practice with logical reasoning, try another set of questions that contain short paragraphs that make a specific argument. Remember that you are looking for the statement that is *best* supported by the information given in the passage.

464. Critical reading is a demanding process. To read critically, you must slow down your reading and, with pencil in hand, perform specific operations on the text. Mark up the text with your reactions, conclusions, and questions. When you read, become an active participant.

This paragraph best supports the statement that
a. critical reading is a slow, dull, but essential process.
b. the best critical reading happens at critical times in a person's life.
c. readers should get in the habit of questioning the truth of what they read.
d. critical reading requires thoughtful and careful attention.
e. critical reading should take place at the same time each day.

465. There are no effective boundaries when it comes to pollutants. Studies have shown that toxic insecticides that have been banned in many countries are riding the wind from countries where they remain legal. Compounds such as DDT and toxaphene have been found in remote places like the Yukon and other Arctic regions.

This paragraph best supports the statement that
a. toxic insecticides such as DDT have not been banned throughout the world.
b. more pollutants find their way into polar climates than they do into warmer areas.
c. studies have proven that many countries have ignored their own anti-pollution laws.
d. DDT and toxaphene are the two most toxic insecticides in the world.
e. even a worldwide ban on toxic insecticides would not stop the spread of DDT pollution.

466. The Fourth Amendment to the Constitution protects citizens against unreasonable searches and seizures. No search of a person's home or personal effects may be conducted without a written search warrant issued on probable cause. This means that a neutral judge must approve the factual basis justifying a search before it can be conducted.

This paragraph best supports the statement that the police cannot search a person's home or private papers unless they have
a. legal authorization.
b. direct evidence of a crime.
c. read the person his or her constitutional rights.
d. a reasonable belief that a crime has occurred.
e. requested that a judge be present.

467. During colonial times in America, juries were encouraged to ask questions of the parties in the courtroom. The jurors were, in fact, expected to investigate the facts of the case themselves. If jurors conducted an investigation today, we would throw out the case.

This paragraph best supports the statement that
a. juries are less important today than they were in colonial times.
b. jurors today are less interested in court cases than they were in colonial times.
c. courtrooms today are more efficient than they were in colonial times.
d. jurors in colonial times were more informed than jurors today.
e. the jury system in America has changed since colonial times.

468. Mathematics allows us to expand our consciousness. Mathematics tells us about economic trends, patterns of disease, and the growth of populations. Math is good at exposing the truth, but it can also perpetuate misunderstandings and untruths. Figures have the power to mislead people.

This paragraph best supports the statement that
a. the study of mathematics is dangerous.
b. words are more truthful than figures.
c. the study of mathematics is more important than other disciplines.
d. the power of numbers is that they cannot lie.
e. figures are sometimes used to deceive people.

469. Human technology developed from the first stone tools about two and a half million years ago. At the beginning the rate of development was slow. Hundreds of thousands of years passed without much change. Today, new technologies are reported daily on television and in newspapers.

The paragraph best supports the statement that
a. stone tools were not really technology.
b. stone tools were in use for two and a half million years.
c. there is no way to know when stone tools first came into use.
d. In today's world, new technologies are constantly being developed.
e. none of the latest technologies are as significant as the development of stone tools.

470. During the past five years, scientists have made significant progress in discovering some of the mechanisms that control human development. They have done this not by studying humans but by studying the development of flies, mice, and other small creatures. Scientists have been able to identify certain genes that become active in these animals' embryos or eggs.

This paragraph best supports the statement that

a. by studying the development of mice, scientists have been able to learn more about human development.

b. scientists have learned to control human development by studying insects and other small animals.

c. certain genes that are active in the embryos of insects have helped scientists to identify the same genes in animals.

d. real progress in the study of human development began only five years ago with the study of small-animal development.

e. scientists became interested in the development of human embryos through their study of the development of smaller creatures.

471. In the 1966 Supreme Court decision *Miranda v. Arizona*, the court held that before the police can obtain statements from a person subjected to an interrogation, the person must be given a *Miranda* warning. This warning means that a person must be told that he or she has the right to remain silent during the police interrogation. Violation of this right means that any statement that the person makes is not admissible in a court hearing.

This paragraph best supports the statement that

a. police who do not warn persons of their *Miranda* rights are guilty of a crime.

b. a *Miranda* warning must be given before a police interrogation can begin.

c. the police may no longer interrogate persons suspected of a crime unless a lawyer is present.

d. the 1966 Supreme Court decision in *Miranda* should be reversed.

e. persons who are interrogated by police should always remain silent until their lawyer comes.

472. Every few decades for more than 150 years, the public library has endured another cycle of change. We're in the middle of one of these cycles today as librarians try to be responsive to the trends of the times. The Internet and CD-ROM technology have had their effect on the public library. This trend is changing libraries in a significant way.

The paragraph best supports the statement that

a. public libraries today are not as responsive to the needs of readers as in past decades.

b. the Internet and CD-ROM should be part of any public library system.

c. new technologies like the Internet and CD-ROM are changing public libraries.

d. librarians are responsible for making the Internet and CD-ROM more popular.

e. widespread use of computers is threatening our public libraries.

473. Desktop videoconferencing may be today's newest meeting technology, but it may not be for everyone. Before you recommend that your company buy a desktop videoconferencing system, you need to examine your goals and needs. New technologies need to complement how people operate within a company.

This paragraph best supports the statement that

a. desktop videoconferencing is the wave of the future for most businesses.

b. before buying a new technology, a company should identify why and how it will be used.

c. new technologies such as desktop videoconferencing are changing the role of the business meeting.

d. how people interrelate within a company is one way of judging whether a company can afford a new technology.

e. many companies cannot afford to buy a desktop videoconferencing system.

SET 34 (Answers begin on page 159.)

Here's one more set of questions based short paragraphs that make a specific argument. You will sometimes have to use inference—reading between the lines—to see which statement is *best* supported by the passage.

474. Electronic mail (e-mail) has been in widespread use for more than a decade. E-mail simplifies the flow of ideas, connects people from distant offices, eliminates the need for meetings, and often boosts productivity. But e-mail should be carefully managed to avoid unclear and inappropriate communication. E-mail messages should be concise and limited to one topic. When complex issues need to be addressed, phone calls are still best.

This paragraph best supports the statement that e-mail
a. is not always the easiest way to connect people from distant offices.
b. has changed considerably since it first began a decade ago.
c. causes people to be unproductive when it is used incorrectly.
d. is most effective when it is used to address uncomplicated matters.
e. is most effective when it is used to address minor matters.

475. During the last six years the number of practicing physicians has increased by about twenty percent. During the same time period, the number of health-care managers has increased by more than six hundred percent. These percentages mean that many doctors have lost the authority to make their own schedules, determine the fees that they charge, and decide on prescribed treatments.

This paragraph best supports the statement that doctors
a. resent the interference of heath-care managers.
b. no longer have adequate training.
c. care a great deal about their patients.
d. are less independent than they used to be.
e. are making a lot less money than they used to make.

476. By the time they reach adulthood, most people can perform many different activities involving motor skills. Motor skills involve such diverse tasks as riding a bicycle, threading a needle, and cooking a dinner. What all these activities have in common is their dependence on precision and timing of muscular movement.

This paragraph best supports the statement that
a. most adults have not refined their motor skills.
b. all adults know how to ride a bicycle.
c. refined motor skills are specifically limited to adults.
d. children perform fewer fine motor activities in a day than adults do.
e. threading a needle is a precise motor skill.

477. Close-up images of Mars by the *Mariner 9* probe indicated networks of valleys that looked like the stream beds on Earth. These images also implied that Mars once had an atmosphere that was thick enough to trap the sun's heat. If this were true, something happened to Mars billions of years ago that stripped away the planet's atmosphere.

This paragraph best supports the statement that
a. Mars now has little or no atmosphere.
b. Mars once had a thicker atmosphere than earth does.
c. the Mariner 9 probe took the first pictures of Mars.
d. Mars is closer to the sun than Earth is.
e. Mars is more mountainous than Earth is.

478. Forest fires feed on decades-long accumulations of debris and leap from the tops of young trees into the branches of mature trees. Fires that jump from treetop to treetop can be devastating. In old-growth forests, however, the shade of mature trees keeps thickets of small trees from sprouting, and the lower branches of mature trees are too high to catch the flames.

This paragraph best supports the statement that
a. forest fire damage is reduced in old-growth forests.
b. small trees should be cut down to prevent forest fires.
c. mature trees should be thinned out to prevent forest fires.
d. forest fires do the most damage in old-growth forests.
e. old-growth forests have a larger accumulation of forest debris.

479. Originating in the 1920s, the Pyramid scheme is one of the oldest con games going. Honest people are often pulled in, thinking the scheme is a legitimate investment enterprise. The first customer to "fall for" the Pyramid scheme will actually make big money and will therefore persuade friends and relatives to join also. The chain then continues with the con artist who originated the scheme pocketing, rather than investing, the money. Finally the pyramid collapses, but by that time the scam artist will usually have moved out of town, leaving no forwarding address.

This paragraph best supports the statement that
a. it is fairly easy to spot a Pyramid scheme in the making.
b. the first customer of a Pyramid scheme is the most gullible.
c. the people who set up Pyramid schemes are able to fool honest people.
d. the Pyramid scheme had its heyday in the 1920s, but it's making a comeback.
e. the Pyramid scheme got its name from its structure.

480. Although romanticized in fiction, the job of a private investigator is often actually boring. The real PI can spend hours or days looking into a not-particularly-lucrative insurance fraud scheme or sitting outside a sleazy motel waiting to catch some not-particularly-attractive philandering husband or wife of a client in the act. In fact, there would be very few private investigators in detective fiction if their jobs had to be portrayed realistically.

This paragraph best supports the statement that private investigators

a. routinely do work related to industrial or family disputes.
b. usually have disreputable clients.
c. embellish their experience so they can write more exciting detective fiction.
d. sometimes choose their line of work because they think it will be romantic.
e. are not usually very well-paid.

481. The motives for skyjacking are as various as the people who commit the crime. Motives may be political or personal, or there may appear to be no motive at all. Skyjackers range from well-organized groups of terrorists to lonely individuals who are mentally ill. Perpetrators may be highly educated or barely able to read; they may be atheists or religious fanatics. This crime is one of the most unpredictable because it is so difficult for law enforcement officials to create an accurate profile of a skyjacker.

This paragraph best supports the statement that

a. people who commit skyjackings are unpredictable.
b. only someone who is emotionally off-balance would commit a skyjacking.
c. creating a good criminal profile depends on the perpetrators having traits in common.
d. skyjackers are particularly difficult to apprehend and prosecute.
e. skyjackers are usually not people who have a fear of flying.

SET 35 (Answers begin on page 160.)

A typical logical reasoning question presents an argument and asks you to analyze it. You may be asked to draw further conclusions from the argument, determine what strengthens or weakens the argument, find flaws in the argument, or justify the argument. Success with these types of questions depends on your being able to understand the structure of the argument. Remember that every argument has a point of view. Every argument draws a conclusion, and is generally supported with evidence. Study each passage so that you can determine how each sentence contributes to the argument the speaker is trying to make. Then make sure you understand the question that is being asked before you choose from the five answer options.

Answer questions 482 and 483 on the basis of the information below.

According to last week's newspaper, doctors in large cities make more money than doctors in small towns or rural areas. It does not seem fair that, just because a doctor's office is in a fancy building or at a fancy address, he or she can charge the patients more. Of course, some medical schools cost more than others, but basically all doctors spend a lot of money and a long time in school. There's no proof that graduates of the more expensive schools practice in big cities and graduates of the less expensive schools practice in small towns. All doctors should charge the same. Whether a patient goes to a doctor in a big city or small town, the cost should be the same.

482. A person seeking to refute the argument might argue that
   a. all doctors charge too much money and should lower their fees.
   b. medical practices are more expensive to maintain in large cities than in small towns and rural areas.
   c. doctors who owe student loans should charge more than other doctors.
   d. medical care from small-town doctors is better than medical care from large-city doctors.
   e. certain medical specialists should charge more than others.

483. A major flaw in the argument is that the speaker assumes that
   a. all doctors are specialists.
   b. all patients carry health insurance.
   c. all doctors have huge student loans.
   d. all patients take too much time.
   e. all doctors see the same number of patients.

Answer questions 484 and 485 on the basis of the information below.

English ought to be the official language of the United States. There is no reason for the government to spend money printing documents in several different languages, just to cater to people who cannot speak English. The government has better ways to spend our money. People who come to this country should learn to speak English right away.

484. Which of the following, if true, would make the speaker's argument stronger?
   a. There is currently a law that says the government must provide people with documents in their native language.
   b. Most people in the United States who do not speak English were born here.
   c. Immigration rates have decreased in recent years.
   d. Many other countries have an official language.
   e. Canada has two official languages.

485. Which of the following, if true, would make the speaker's argument weaker?
   a. The government currently translates official documents into more than twenty languages.
   b. English is the most difficult language in the world to learn.
   c. Most people who immigrate to the United States learn English within two years of their arrival.
   d. Making English the official language is a politically unpopular idea.
   e. People who are bilingual are usually highly educated.

Answer questions 486 through 488 on the basis of the information below.

Some groups want to outlaw burning the flag. They say that people have fought and died for the flag and that citizens of the United States ought to respect that. But I say that respect cannot be legislated. Also, most citizens who have served in the military did not fight for the flag, they fought for what the flag represents. Among the things the flag represents is freedom of speech, which includes, I believe, the right for a citizen to express displeasure with the government by burning the flag in protest.

486. Which of the following best expresses the main point of the passage?
   a. Only veterans care about the flag-burning issue.
   b. Flag burning almost never happens, so outlawing it is a waste of time.
   c. Flag burning will be a very important issue in the next election.
   d. To outlaw flag burning is to outlaw what the flag represents.
   e. Burning the flag should only be illegal when it is done in foreign countries.

487. Which of the following, if true, would weaken the speaker's argument?
   a. An action is not considered a part of freedom of speech.
   b. People who burn the flag usually commit other crimes as well.
   c. The flag was not recognized by the government until 1812.
   d. State flags are almost never burned.
   e. Most people are against flag burning.

488. Which of the following is similar to the argument made by the speaker?

    a. The rich should not be allowed to "buy" politicians, so the Congress should enact campaign finance reform.

    b. The idea of freedom of religion also means the right not to participate in religion, so mandated school prayer violates freedom of religion.

    c. The Constitution guarantees freedom to own property, so taxes should be illegal.

    d. Convicted felons should not have their convictions overturned on a technicality.

    e. In order to understand what may be constitutional today, one needs to look at what the laws were when the Constitution was enacted.

SET 36 (Answers begin on page 161.)

Some logical reasoning questions ask you to determine the method the speaker is using when he or she presents the argument. Method-of-argument questions ask you to demonstrate an understanding of how a speaker's argument is put together. To determine the method of argument, again focus on the conclusion and on the evidence presented. What method does the speaker use to link the two?

Answer question 489 on the basis of the information below.

I know that our rules prohibit members from bringing more than one guest at a time to the club, but I think there should be an exception to the rule on Tuesdays, Wednesdays, and Thursdays. Members should be allowed to bring multiple guests on those days, since the majority of members use the club facilities on the other four days of the week.

489. The rules restricting the number of guests a member can bring to the club probably are intended to
a. assure that members are not crowded by the presence of guests.
b. provide extra income for the club on slow days.
c. allow members to bring guests to the club for special events.
d. restrict guests to public areas of the club.
e. control the exact number of people in the club at any time.

Answer questions 490 and 491 on the basis of the information below.

A recent study on professional football players showed that this new ointment helps relieve joint pain. My mother has arthritis, and I told her she should try it, but she says it probably won't help her.

490. What argument should Mother use to point out why the ointment probably will not help her arthritis?
a. The ointment was just experimental.
b. The ointment is expensive.
c. Football players' joint pain is not the result of arthritis.
d. She has already tried another ointment and it didn't work.
e. Football players are generally younger than she is.

491. Which of the following, if true, would strengthen the speaker's argument?
a. Mother used to be a professional bowler.
b. Football players' injuries are rarely painful.
c. Mother's arthritis only flares up in bad weather.
d. Mother finds exercise helps her arthritis.
e. Football players who are injured tend to develop arthritis.

Answer questions 492 through 494 on the basis of the information below.

Giving children computers in grade school is a waste of money and teachers' time. These children are too young to learn how to use computers effectively and need to spend time on learning the basics, like arithmetic and reading. After all, a baby has to crawl before she can walk.

492. Which of the following methods of argument is used in the above passage?
   a. a specific example that illustrates the speaker's point
   b. attacking the beliefs of those who disagree with the speaker
   c. relying on an analogy to prove the speaker's point
   d. displaying statistics that back up the speaker's point
   e. comparing different methods of learning

493. Which of the following, if true, would strengthen the speaker's argument?
   a. studies showing computers are expensive
   b. research on the effect of computer games on children
   c. examples of high school students who use computers improperly
   d. proof that the cost of computers is coming down
   e. evidence that using computers makes learning to read difficult

494. Which of the following, if true, would weaken the speaker's argument?
   a. a demonstration that computers can be used to teach reading and arithmetic
   b. analysis of the cost-effectiveness of new computers versus repairing old computers
   c. examples of adults who do not know how to use computers
   d. recent grade reports of students in the computer classes
   e. a visit to a classroom where computers are being used

Answer questions 495 and 496 on the basis of the information below.

The corner of Elm and Third needs to have a stoplight. Children cross this intersection on the way to school and sometimes they do not check for traffic. I've seen several children almost get hit by cars at this corner. I know that stoplights are not cheap, and I know that children cannot be protected from every danger, but this is one of the worst intersections in town. There needs to be a stop light here so that traffic will be slowed down and the children can walk more safely.

495. Which of the following methods of argument is used in the above passage?
   a. analogy—comparing the intersection to something dangerous
   b. emotion—referring to the safety of children to get people interested
   c. statistical analysis—noting the number of children almost hit and the cost of a stop light
   d. personalization—telling the story of one child's near accident at the intersection
   e. attack—pointing out that people who are against the stoplight do not care about children

496. Which of the following, if true, would weaken the speaker's argument?
   a. Sometimes cars run red lights.
   b. Fewer children are injured at corners that have stoplights.
   c. If parents teach their children basic traffic safety, then they might remember to look for cars.
   d. Children from this neighborhood used to take the bus to a school farther away.
   e. In the last year, there have only been three minor accidents at the intersection and none of them involved children.

SET 37 (Answers begin on page 162.)

Another type of logical reasoning question presents you with two different speakers talking about the same issue. Sometimes the speakers' arguments overlap; in other words, they support each other. Sometimes the speakers are presenting opposing viewpoints. For these items, make sure you understand the conclusion of *both* speakers before you attempt to answer the questions.

Answer questions 497 and 498 on the basis of the information below.

> *Frances:* Studies show that eating a healthy breakfast improves young children's ability to learn. However, it is not the responsibility of the schools to provide this meal; it is the responsibility of each child's parents.

> *Lars:* Although it would be nice if the schools could provide each child with a healthy breakfast, the cost of doing that takes money away from other, more important learning resources, such as the purchase of new computers. In the long run, children learn more when the schools concentrate on the services they traditionally provide and the parents do what they are supposed to do.

497. In what way does Lars's comment relate to Frances's?
   a. It weakens Frances's argument by changing the focus of the discussion.
   b. It strengthens Frances's argument by providing support for her premise.
   c. It states the logical outcome of Frances's views.
   d. It cannot be true if Frances's assertion about parental responsibility is true.
   e. It provides an argument that is the opposite of Frances's views.

498. What main assumption underlies each statement?
   a. As teachers become more scarce, schools will have to learn to be more cost-effective in recruiting new teachers.
   b. In the information age, the equipment schools must purchase for their students is getting more expensive.
   c. The study about students and breakfast is inconclusive at best, and more studies should be conducted to find out if school breakfasts are healthy.
   d. Schools have never had the responsibility for supplying students with breakfast; rather, they spend their money on teachers, books, and other tangibles of education.
   e. Parents are not assuming enough responsibility for their children's education and should become more involved in school issues.

Answer questions 499 through 501 on the basis of the information below.

Quinn: Our state is considering raising the age at which a person can get a driver's license to eighteen. This is unfair because the age has been sixteen for many years and sixteen-year-olds today are no less responsible than their parents and grandparents were at sixteen. Many young people today who are fourteen and fifteen years old are preparing to receive their licenses by driving with a learner's permit and a licensed driver, usually one of their parents. It would not be fair to suddenly say they have to wait two more years.

Dakota: It is true that people have been allowed to receive a driver's license at sixteen for generations. However, in recent years, the increase in traffic means drivers face more dangers than ever and must be ready to respond to a variety of situations. The fact that schools can no longer afford to teach drivers' education results in too many young drivers who are not prepared to face the traffic conditions of today.

499. What is the point at issue between Quinn and Dakota?
  a. whether sixteen-year-olds should be required to take drivers' education before being issued a license
  b. whether schools ought to provide drivers' education to fourteen- and fifteen-year-old students
  c. whether the standards for issuing drivers' licenses should become more stringent
  d. whether sixteen-year-olds are prepared to drive in today's traffic conditions
  e. whether parents are able to do a good job teaching their children to drive

500. On what does Quinn rely in making her argument?
  a. statistics
  b. emotion
  c. fairness
  d. anecdotes
  e. actualities

501. On what does Dakota rely in making her argument?
  a. statistics
  b. emotion
  c. fairness
  d. anecdotes
  e. actualities

ANSWERS

SET 1 (Page 6)

1. **b.** This is a simple addition series. Each number increases by 3.
2. **a.** This is a simple subtraction series; each number is 7 less than the previous number.
3. **c.** This is an alternation with repetition series in which each number repeats itself, and then increases by 6.
4. **d.** In this addition series, 1 is added to the first number; 2 is added to the second number; 3 is added to the third number; and so forth.
5. **a.** This is a simple subtraction series; each number is 25 less than the previous number.
6. **a.** This is an alternating addition and subtraction series. In the first pattern, 10 is subtracted from each number to arrive at the next. In the second, 5 is added to each number to arrive at the next.
7. **d.** This is a simple addition series with a random number, 9, interpolated as every other number. In the series, 6 is added to each number except 9, to arrive at the next number.
8. **b.** This is an alternating subtraction series. First 2 is subtracted, then 4, then 2, and so on.
9. **c.** In this simple alternating addition and subtraction series, 2 is subtracted, then 1 is added, and so on.
10. **d.** This alternating addition series begins with 3; then 1 is added to give 4; then 3 is added to give 7; then 1 is added, and so on.
11. **a.** This is a simple alternating subtraction series, which subtracts 2, then 5.

12. **c.** In this alternating repetition series, the random number 21 is interpolated every other number into an otherwise simple addition series that increases by 2, beginning with the number 9.

13. **b.** In this series, each number is repeated, then 13 is subtracted to arrive at the next number.

14. **c.** This is a simple multiplication series. Each number is 3 times more than the previous number.

15. **a.** This is a simple division series. Each number is divided by 5.

16. **b.** This is a simple alternating addition and subtraction series. In the first pattern, 3 is added; in the second, 2 is subtracted.

17. **b.** This is an alternating multiplication and subtracting series: First, multiply by 2, and then subtract 8.

18. **c.** In this simple addition series, each number increases by 0.8.

19. **d.** In this simple subtraction series, each number decreases by 0.4.

20. **b.** This is a simple division series; each number is one-half of the previous number.

SET 2 (Page 8)

21. d. In this simple subtraction series, each number is 8 less than the previous number.

22. b. In this simple addition series, each number is 5 greater than the previous number.

23. e. This is a simple subtraction with repetition series. It begins with 19, which is repeated, then 2 is subtracted, resulting in 17, which is repeated, and so on.

24. e. This is a simple addition series with a random number, 21, interpolated as every third number. In the series, 6 is added to each number except 21, to arrive at the next number.

25. a. In this alternating repetition series, a random number, 33, is interpolated every third number into a simple addition series, in which each number increases by 2.

26. b. This is a simple addition series, which begins with 2 and adds 6.

27. a. This is an alternating subtraction series with the interpolation of a random number, 5, as every third number. In the subtraction series, 3 is subtracted, then 4, then 3, and so on.

28. e. This is a simple alternating addition and subtraction series. First, 3 is added, then 1 is subtracted; then 3 is added, 1 subtracted, and so on.

29. b. This is a simple subtraction series in which a random number, 85, is interpolated as every third number. In the subtraction series, 10 is subtracted from each number to arrive at the next.

30. c. Here every other number follows a different pattern. In the first series, 6 is added to each number to arrive at the next. In the second series, 10 is added to each number to arrive at the next.

31. e. This is an alternating addition series, in which 10 is added, then 5, then 10, and so on.

32. a. This is a subtraction series with repetition. Each number repeats itself and then decreases by 9.

33. e. This is an alternating subtraction series with repetition. There are two different patterns here. In the first, a number repeats itself; then 3 is added to that number to arrive at the next number, which also repeats. This gives the series 17, 17, 20, 20, 23, and so on. Every third number follows a second pattern, in which 3 is subtracted from each number to arrive at the next: 34, 31, 28.

34. d. This is an alternating addition series, with a random number, 4, interpolated as every third number. In the main series 1 is added, then 2 is added, then 1, then 2, and so on.

35. e. This is an alternating repetition series, in which a random number, 61, is interpolated as every third number into an otherwise simple subtraction series. Starting with the second number, 57, each number (except 61) is 7 less than the previous number.

36. d. Here is a simple addition series, which begins with 9 and adds 7.

37. **c.** This is an alternating repetition series, with a random number, 22, interpolated as every third number into an otherwise simple addition series. In the addition series, 4 is added to each number to arrive at the next number.

38. **d.** This is an alternating addition and subtraction series. In the first pattern, 2 is added to each number to arrive at the next; in the alternate pattern, 4 is subtracted from each number to arrive at the next.

39. **d.** In this simple addition series, each number is 4 more than the previous number.

40. **b.** This is an alternating addition series, with a random number, 19, interpolated as every third number. The addition series alternates between adding 3 and adding 4. The number 19 appears after each number arrived at by adding 3.

SET 3 (Page 10)

41. **e.** This is a simple subtraction series, in which 3 is subtracted from each number to arrive at the next.

42. **e.** This simple addition series adds 4 to each number to arrive at the next.

43. **d.** This is a simple subtraction series, in which 4 is subtracted from each number to arrive at the next.

44. **d.** Here are two alternating patterns, one addition and one subtraction. The first starts with 2 and increases by 2; the second starts with 44 and decreases by 3.

45. **a.** In this simple subtraction series, the numbers decrease by 3.

46. **b.** In this simple addition with repetition series, each number in the series repeats itself, and then increases by 11 to arrive at the next number.

47. **b.** This is an alternating addition and subtraction series, in which the addition of 5 is alternated with the subtraction of 3.

48. **e.** Two patterns alternate here, with every third number following the alternate pattern. In the main series, beginning with 2, 3 is added to each number to arrive at the next. In the alternating series, beginning with 28, 8 is subtracted from each number to arrive at the next.

49. **c.** This is an alternating addition series that adds 5, then 2, then 5, and so on.

50. **d.** In this simple subtraction with repetition series, each number is repeated, then 3 is subtracted to give the next number, which is then repeated, and so on.

51. **b.** Here there are two alternating patterns, with every other number following a different pattern. The first pattern begins with 13 and adds 2 to each number to arrive at the next; the alternat-

ing pattern begins with 29 and subtracts 3 each time.

52. **c.** Here every third number follows a different pattern from the main series. In the main series, beginning with 16, 10 is added to each number to arrive at the next. In the alternating series, beginning with 56, 12 is added to each number to arrive at the next.

53. **a.** This is an alternating addition series with repetition, in which a random number, 66, is interpolated as every third number. The regular series adds 2, then 3, then 2, and so on, with 66 repeated after each "add 2" step.

54. **c.** This is an alternating addition series, with a random number, 35, interpolated as every third number. The pattern of addition is to add 2, add 5, add 2, and so on. The number 35 comes after each "add 2" step.

55. **e.** This is an alternating subtraction series, which subtracts 5, then 2, then 5, and so on.

56. **c.** This is an alternating subtraction series in which 2 is subtracted twice, then 3 is subtracted once, then 2 is subtracted twice, and so on.

57. **a.** This is a simple addition series with repetition. It adds 3 to each number to arrive at the next, which is repeated before 3 is added again.

58. **c.** Here are two alternating patterns. The first begins with 17 and adds 2; the second begins with 32 and subtracts 3.

59. **a.** Two patterns alternate here. The first pattern begins with 10 and adds 2 to each number to arrive at the next; the alternating pattern begins with 34 and subtracts 3 each time.

60. **a.** This is an alternating repetition series. The number 32 alternates with a series in which each number decreases by 2.

SET 4 (Page 12)

61. **a.** This is a simple alternating addition and subtraction series. The first series begins with 10 and adds 2; the second begins with 34 and subtracts 3.

62. **d.** In this simple addition with repetition series, each number in the series repeats itself, and then increases by 11 to arrive at the next number.

63. **b.** This is a simple subtraction series in which a random number, 85, is interpolated as every third number. In the subtraction series, 10 is subtracted from each number to arrive at the next.

64. **a.** Two series alternate here, with every third number following a different pattern. In the main series, 3 is added to each number to arrive at the next. In the alternating series, 8 is subtracted from each number to arrive at the next.

65. **d.** This series alternates the addition of 5 with the subtraction of 3.

66. **a.** In this series, 5 is added to the previous number; the number 70 is inserted as every third number.

67. **d.** This is an alternating division and addition series: First, divide by 2, and then add 8.

68. **c.** This is a simple multiplication series. Each number is 2 times greater than the previous number.

69. **b.** This is a multiplication series; each number is 3 times the previous number.

70. **a.** In this series, the letters progress by 1; the numbers decrease by 3.

71. **b.** In this series, the letters progress by 2, and the numbers increase by 2.

72. **c.** The letters decrease by 1; the numbers are multiplied by 2.

73. **d.** This is a simple addition series; each number is 3 more than the previous number.

74. **c.** This is a simple subtraction series; each number is 4 less than the previous number.

75. **b.** This is an alternating addition and subtraction series. Roman numbers alternate with Arabic numbers. In the Roman numeral pattern, each number decreases by 1. In the Arabic numeral pattern, each number increases by 1.

SET 5 (Page 14)

76. **a.** This series consists of letters in a reverse alphabetical order.

77. **b.** This is an alternating series in alphabetical order. The middle letters follow the order ABCDE. The first and third letters are alphabetical beginning with J. The third letter is repeated as a first letter in each subsequent three-letter segment.

78. **b.** Because the letters are the same, concentrate on the number series, which is a simple 2, 3, 4, 5, 6 series, and follows each letter in order.

79. **d.** The second and forth letters in the series, L and A, are static. The first and third letters consist of an alphabetical order beginning with the letter E.

80. **c.** The first two letters, PQ, are static. The third letter is in alphabetical order, beginning with R. The number series is in descending order beginning with 5.

81. **c.** The first letters are in alphabetical order with a letter skipped in between each segment: C, E, G, I, K. The second and third letters are repeated; they are also in order with a skipped letter: M, O, Q, S, U.

82. **a.** In this series, the third letter is repeated as the first letter of the next segment. The middle letter, A, remains static. The third letters are in alphabetical order, beginning with R.

83. **d.** In this series, the letters remain the same: DEF. The subscript numbers follow this series: 1,1,1; 1,1,2; 1,2,2; 2,2,2; 2,2,3.

84. **c.** There are two alphabetical series here. The first series is with the first letters only: VWXYZ. The second series involves the remaining letters: AB, CD, EF, GH, IJ.

85. **a.** The middle letters are static, so concentrate on the first and third letters. The series involves an alphabetical order with a reversal of the letters. The first letters are in alphabetical order: B, C, D, E, F. The second and forth segments are reversals of the first and third segments. The missing segment begins with a new letter.

86. **a.** This series consists of a simple alphabetical order with the first two letters of all segments: L, M, N, O, P, Q, R, S, T, U. The third letter of each segment is a repetition of the first letter.

87. **d.** There are three series to look for here. The first letters are alphabetical in reverse: Z, Y, X, W, V. The second letters are in alphabetical order, beginning with A. The number series is as follows: 5, 4, 6, 3, 7.

SET 6 (Page 15)

88. **b.** Look at each segment. In the first segment, the arrows are both pointing to the right. In the second segment, the first arrow is up and the second is down. The third segment repeats the first segment. In the fourth segment, the arrows are up and then down. Because this is an alternating series, the two arrows pointing right will be repeated, so option **b** is the only possible choice.

89. **b.** Notice that in each segment, the figures are all the same shape, but the one in the middle is larger than the two on either side. Also, notice that one of the figures is shaded and that this shading alternates first right and then left. To continue this pattern in the third segment, you will look for a square. Choice **b** is correct because this choice will put the large square between the two smaller squares, with the shading on the right.

90. **c.** This is an alternating series. In the first segment, the letter "E" faces right, then down, then right. In the second segment, the letters all face down. To follow this pattern, in the fourth segment, the letters must all face up.

91. **c.** In this series, the shaded part inside the circle gets larger and then smaller.

92. **d.** Look for opposites in this series of figures. The first and second segments are opposites of each other. The same is true for the third and fourth segments.

93. **a.** Look carefully at the number of dots in each domino-like figure. The first segment goes from five to three to one. The second segment goes from one to three to five. The third segment repeats the first segment.

94. **c.** All four segments use the same figures: two squares, one circle, and one triangle. In the first segment, the squares are on the outside of the circle and triangle. In the second segment, the squares are below the other two. In the third segment, the squares on are the inside. In the fourth segment, the squares are above the triangle and circle.

95. **a.** Look at each segment. You will notice that in each, the figure on the right and the figure on the left are the same; the figure in between is different. To continue this pattern in the last segment, the diamond on the left will be repeated on the right. Choice **a** is the only possible answer.

96. **b.** Each arrow in this continuing series moves a few degrees in a clockwise direction. Think of these arrows as the big hand on a clock. The first arrow is at noon. The last arrow before the blank would be 12:40. Choice **b**, the correct answer, is at 12:45.

97. **c.** Study the pattern carefully. In the first segment, two letters face right and the next two face left. The first letter in the second segment repeats the last letter of the previous segment. The same is true for the third segment. But the forth segment changes again; it is the opposite of the first segment, so the last two letters must face right.

98. **d.** This sequence concerns the number of sides on each figure. In the first segment, the three figures have one side, and then two sides, and then three sides. In the second segment, the number of sides increases and then decreases. In the third segment, the number of sides continues to decrease.

99. **a.** In this series the figures increase the amount of shading by one-fourth and, once a square is completely shaded, starts over with an unshaded square. In the second segment, you will notice that the figure goes from completely shaded to completely unshaded. This is why choice **a** is the correct choice.

100. **d.** This is an alternating series. The first and third segments are repeated. The second segment is simply upside down.

101. **d.** In each of the segments the figures alternate between one-half and one-fourth shaded.

SET 7 (Page 17)

102. c. A leopard, a cougar, and a lion all belong to the cat family; an elephant does not.

103. b. The couch, table, and chair are pieces of furniture; the rug is not.

104. a. The yarn, the twine, and the cord are all used for tying. The tape is not used in the same way.

105. b. The flute, saxophone, and trumpet are wind instruments; the violin is a stringed instrument.

106. d. Sleeve, pocket, and collar are all parts of a shirt.

107. c. Pecans, walnuts, and cashews are all types of nuts. A kernel is not a type of nut.

108. d. Rayon, silk, and cotton are all types of fabric. Cloth is not a fabric type.

109. b. The roof, door, and window are parts of a house. The sidewalk is in front of the house, but it is not part of the building.

110. d. The first three choices are all synonyms.

111. a. The index, the glossary, and the chapters are all parts of a book. Choice **a** does not belong because the book is the whole, not a part.

112. c. The noun, the preposition, and the adverb are classes of words that make up a sentence. Punctuation belongs in a sentence, but punctuation is not a class of word.

113. d. The cornea, retina, and pupil are all parts of the eye.

114. d. Rye, sourdough, and pumpernickel are types of bread. A loaf is not a bread type.

115. b. An ounce measures weight; the other choices measure length.

116. a. Freeway, interstate, and expressway are all high-speed highways; a street is for low-speed traffic.

117. b. *Dodge, duck,* and *avoid* are all synonyms meaning *evade. Flee* means to *run away from.*

118. c. Heading, body, and closing are all parts of a letter; the letter is the whole, not a part.

SET 8 (Page 19)

119. **d.** The core, the seeds, and the pulp are all parts of an apple. A slice would be a piece taken out of an apple.

120. **b.** *Festive, joyous,* and *merry* are all synonyms. *Lucky* has a different meaning.

121. **c.** Geology, zoology, and botany are all branches of science. Theology is the study of religion.

122. **a.** The parallelogram, the square, and the rectangle all have four sides. The sphere is a different shape and has no angles.

123. **a.** *Falter, hesitate,* and *waver* are all synonyms; *baffle* does not mean the same thing.

124. **d.** *Instruct, teach,* and *educate* are all synonyms.

125. **a.** The trout, sardine, and catfish are all types of fish; the lobster is a crustacean.

126. **c.** The scythe, the knife, and the saw are all cutting tools. Pliers are tools but they are not used for cutting.

127. **b.** Two, six, and eight are all even numbers; three is an odd number.

128. **c.** A peninsula, an island, and a cape are all landforms; a bay is a body of water.

129. **c.** Seat, rung, and leg are all parts of a chair. Not all chairs have cushions.

130. **d.** *Fair, just,* and *equitable* are all synonyms meaning *impartial. Favorable* means *expressing approval.*

131. **c.** Defendant, prosecutor, and judge are all persons involved in a trial. A trial is not a person.

132. **b.** *Area, circumference,* and *quadrilateral* are all terms used in the study of geometry. *Variable* is a term generally used in the study of algebra.

133. **b.** The mayor, governor, and senator are all persons elected to government offices; the lawyer is not an elected official.

134. **d.** *Acute, right,* and *obtuse* are geometric terms describing particular angles. *Parallel* refers to two lines that never intersect.

135. **c.** The wing, fin, and rudder are all parts of an airplane.

136. **a.** The heart, liver, and stomach are all organs of the body. The aorta is an artery, not an organ.

SET 9 (Page 21)

137. **b.** The necessary part of a book is its pages; there is no book without pages. Not all books are fiction (choice **a**), and not all books have pictures (choice **c**). Learning (choice **d**) may or may not take place with a book.

138. **d.** A piano does not exist without a keyboard, so the keyboard is an essential part of a piano. An orchestra is not necessary to a piano (choice **a**). Notes are byproducts of a piano (choice **b**). Piano playing can be learned without a teacher (choice **c**).

139. **a.** All shoes have a sole of some sort. Not all shoes are made of leather (choice **b**); nor do they all have laces (choice **c**). Walking (choice **d**) is not essential to a shoe.

140. **c.** A person or animal must take in oxygen for respiration to occur. A mouth (choice **a**) is not essential because breathing can occur through the nose. Choices **b** and **d** are clearly not essential and can be ruled out.

141. **b.** An election does not exist without voters. The election of a president (choice **a**) is a byproduct. Not all elections are held in November (choice **c**), nor are they nationwide (choice **d**).

142. **d.** A diploma is awarded at graduation, so graduation is essential to obtaining a diploma. Employment may be a byproduct (choice **c**). A principal and a curriculum (choices **a** and **b**) may play a role in the awarding of some diplomas, but they are not essential.

143. **c.** The necessary part of a lake is its water; without water there is no lake. The other choices are elements that may or may not be present.

144. **a.** Without soldiers, an army cannot exist; therefore, the soldiers are the essential part of an army. The other choices may be related, but they are not essential.

145. **d.** Words are a necessary part of language. Slang is not necessary to language (choice **b**). Not all languages are written (choice **c**). Words do not have to be spoken in order to be part of a language (choice **a**).

146. **b.** A desert is an arid tract of land. Not all deserts are flat (choice **d**). Not all deserts have cacti or oases (choices **a** and **c**).

147. **a.** Lightning is produced from a discharge of electricity, so electricity is essential. Thunder and rain are not essential to the production of lightning (choices **b** and **d**). Brightness may be a byproduct of lightning, but it is not essential (choice **c**).

148. **b.** The essential part of a monopoly is that it involves exclusive ownership or control.

149. **d.** In order to harvest something, one must have a crop, which is the essential element for this item. Autumn (choice **a**) is not the only time that crops are harvested. There may not be enough of a crop to stockpile (choice **b**), and crops may be harvested without a tractor (choice **c**).

150. **a.** A gala indicates a celebration, the necessary element here. A tuxedo (choice **b**) is not required garb at a gala, nor is an appetizer (choice **c**) needed. A gala may be held without the benefit of anyone speaking (choice **d**).

151. **d.** Pain is suffering or hurt, so choice **d** is the essential element. Without hurt, there is no pain. A cut (choice **a**) or a burn (choice **b**) may cause pain, but so do many other types of injury. A nuisance (choice **c**) is an annoyance that may cause pain, but not necessarily.

SET 10 (Page 23)

152. **c.** An infirmary is a place for the care of the infirm, sick, or injured. Without patients, there is no infirmary. Surgery (choice **a**) may not be required for patients. A disease (choice **b**) is not necessary because the infirmary may only see patients with injuries. A receptionist (choice **d**) would be helpful but not essential.

153. **b.** A facsimile must involve an image of some sort. The image or facsimile need not, however, be a picture. A mimeograph and a copier machine are just a two of the ways that images may be produced, so they do not qualify as the essential element for this item.

154. **b.** A domicile is a legal residence, so dwelling is the essential component for this item. You do not need a tenant (choice **a**) in the domicile, nor do you have to have a kitchen (choice **c**). A house (choice **d**) is just one form of a domicile (which could also be a tent, hogan, van, camper, motor home, apartment, dormitory, etc.).

155. **d.** A culture is the behavior pattern of a particular population, so customs are the essential element. A culture may or may not be civil or educated (choices **a** and **b**). A culture may be an agricultural society (choice **c**), but this is not the essential element.

156. **a.** A bonus is something given or paid beyond what is usual or expected, so reward is the essential element. A bonus may not involve a raise in pay or cash (choices **b** and **c**), and it may be received from someone other than an employer (choice **d**).

157. **c.** An antique is something that is belonging to, or made in, an earlier period. It may or may not be a rarity (choice **a**), and it does not have to be an artifact, an object produced or shaped by human craft (choice **b**). An antique is old but does not have to be prehistoric (choice **d**).

158. **b.** An itinerary is a proposed route of a journey. A map (choice **a**) is not necessary to have a planned route. Travel (choice **c**) is *usually* the outcome of an itinerary, but not always. A guidebook (choice **d**) may be used to plan the journey but is not essential.

159. **c.** An orchestra is a large group of musicians, so musicians are essential. Although many orchestras have violin sections, violins aren't essential to an orchestra (choice **a**). Neither a stage (choice **b**) nor a soloist (choice **d**) is necessary.

160. **d.** Knowledge is understanding gained through experience or study, so learning is the essential element. A school (choice **a**) is not necessary for learning or knowledge to take place, nor is a teacher or a textbook (choices **b** and **c**).

161. **d.** A dimension is a measure of spatial content. A compass (choice **a**) and ruler (choice **b**) may help to determine the dimension, but other instruments may also be used, so these are not the essential element here. An inch (choice **c**) is only one way to determine a dimension.

162. **a.** Sustenance is something, especially food, that sustains life or health, so nourishment is the essential element. Water and grains (choices **b** and **c**) are components of nourishment, but other things can be taken in as well. A menu (choice **d**) may present a list of foods but is not essential to sustenance.

163. **c.** An ovation is prolonged, enthusiastic applause, so applause is necessary to an ovation. An outburst (choice **a**) may take place during an ovation, "bravo" (choice **b**) may or may not be uttered, and an encore (choice **d**) would take place *after* an ovation.

164. **a.** All vertebrates have a backbone. Reptiles (choice **b**) are vertebrates, but so are many other animals. Mammals (choice **c**) are vertebrates, but so are birds and reptiles. All vertebrates (choice **d**) are animals, but not all animals are vertebrates.

165. **b.** Provisions imply the general supplies that are needed, so choice **b** is the essential element. The other choices are byproducts, but they are not essential.

166. **d.** A purchase is an acquisition of something. A purchase may be made by trade (choice **a**) or with money (choice **b**), so those are not essential elements. A bank (choice **c**) may or may not be involved in a purchase.

SET 11 (Page 25)

167. **a.** A dome is a large rounded roof or ceiling, so being rounded is essential to a dome. A geodesic dome (choice **b**) is only one type of dome. Some, but not all domes, have copper roofs (choice **d**). Domes are often found on government buildings (choice **c**), but domes exist in many other places.

168. **b.** A recipe is a list of directions to make something. Recipes may be used to prepare food (choice **a**), among other things. One does not need a cookbook (choice **c**) to have a recipe, and utensils (choice **d**) may or may not be used to make a recipe.

169. **d.** A hurricane cannot exist without wind. A beach is not essential to a hurricane (choice **a**). A hurricane is a type of cyclone, which rules out choice **b**. Not all hurricanes cause damage (choice **c**).

170. **c.** Without a signature, there is no autograph. Athletes and actors (choices **a** and **b**) may sign autographs, but they are not essential. An autograph can be signed with something other than a pen (choice **d**).

171. **a.** Residents must be present in order to have a town. A town may be too small to have skyscrapers (choice **b**). A town may or may not have parks (choice **c**) and libraries (choice **d**), so they are not the essential elements.

172. **d.** A wedding results in a joining, or a marriage, so choice **d** is the essential element. Love (choice **a**) usually precedes a wedding, but it is not essential. A wedding may take place anywhere, so a church (choice **b**) is not required. A ring (choice **c**) is often used in a wedding, but it is not necessary.

173. **c.** A faculty is made up of a group of teachers and cannot exist without them. The faculty may work in buildings (choice **a**), but the buildings aren't essential. They may use textbooks (choice **b**) and attend meetings (choice **d**), but these aren't essential either.

174. **a.** A cage is meant to keep something surrounded, so enclosure is the essential element. A prisoner (choice **b**) or an animal (choice **c**) are two things that may be kept in cages, among many other things. A zoo (choice **d**) is only one place that has cages.

175. **b.** A directory is a listing of names or things, so choice **b** is the essential element. A telephone (choice **a**) often has a directory associated with it, but is not essential. A computer (choice **c**) uses a directory format to list files, but is not required. Names (choice **d**) are often listed in a directory, but many other things are listed in directories, so this is not the essential element.

176. **a.** An agreement is necessary in order to have a contract. A contract may appear on a document (choice **b**), but it is not required. A contract may be oral as well as written, so choice **c** is not essential. A contract can be made without an attorney (choice **d**).

177. **b.** A saddle is something one uses to sit on an animal, so it must have a seat (choice **b**). A saddle often is used on a horse (choice **a**), but may be used on other animals. Stirrups (choice **c**) are often found on a saddle but may not be used. A horn (choice **d**) is found on Western saddles, but not English saddles, so it is not the essential element here.

178. **a.** Something cannot vibrate without creating motion, so motion is essential to vibration.

179. **b.** The essential part of a cell is its nucleus. Not all cells produce chlorophyll (choice **a**). Not all cells are nerve cells (choice **c**). All living things, not just humans (choice **d**), have cells.

180. **c.** Without a first-place win there is no champion, so winning is essential. There may be champions in running, swimming, or speaking, but there are also champions in many other areas.

181. **d.** A glacier is a large mass of ice, and cannot exist without it. A glacier can move down a mountain, but it can also move across a valley or a plain, which rules out choice **a**. Glaciers exist in all seasons, which rules out choice **b**. There are many glaciers in the world today, which rules out choice **c**.

SET 12 (Page 27)

182. **b.** Coffee goes into a cup and soup goes into a bowl. Choices **a** and **c** are incorrect because they are other utensils. The answer is not choice **d** because the word *food* is too general.

183. **d.** The telephone is a means of communication. The bus is a means of transportation. Aviation (choice **a**) is not the answer because it is a type of transportation, not a means. The answer is not choice **b** or choice **c** because neither of these represents a means of transportation.

184. **c.** A bicycle is put in motion by means of a pedal. A canoe is put into motion by means of an oar. The answer is not choice **a** because the substance water does not necessarily put the canoe into motion. Kayak (choice **b**) is incorrect because it is a type of boat similar to a canoe. Choice **d** is incorrect because a fleet is a group of boats.

185. **d.** A window is made up of panes, and a book is made up of pages. The answer is not choice **a,** because a novel is a type of book. The answer is not choice **b,** because glass has no relationship to a book. Choice **c** is incorrect because a cover is only one part of a book; a book is not made up of covers.

186. **c.** *Scarcely* is the opposite of *mostly,* and *quietly* is the opposite of *loudly.* Choices **a** and **b** are clearly not opposites of quietly. Choice **d** means the same as quietly.

187. **b.** A baker makes bread; a congressman makes laws. The answer is not choice **a,** because a senator and a congressman both make laws. Choice **c** is incorrect because a congressman does not make a state. Politician (choice **d**) is also incorrect because a congressman is a politician.

188. **b.** An actor performs in a play. A musician performs at a concert. Choices **a, c,** and **d** are incorrect because none are people who perform.

189. **a.** *Tactful* and *diplomatic* are synonyms (they mean about the same thing). *Bashful* and *timid* are also synonyms. The answer is not choice **b** or **c** because neither of these means the same as *bashful.* Choice **d** is incorrect because *bold* means the opposite of *bashful.*

190. **d.** A group of lions is called a pride. A group of fish swim in a school. Teacher (choice **a**) and student (choice **b**) refer to another meaning of the word *school.* The answer is not choice **c** because self-respect has no obvious relationship to this particular meaning of school.

191. **a.** *Control* and *dominate* are synonyms, and *magnify* and *enlarge* are synonyms. The answer is not choice **b** or **d** because neither of these means the same as *enlarge.* Choice **c** is incorrect because *decrease* is the opposite of *enlarge.*

192. **b.** A yard is a larger measure than an inch (a yard contains 36 inches). A quart is a larger measure than an ounce (a quart contains 32 ounces). Gallon (choice **a**) is incorrect because it is larger than a quart. Choices **c** and **d** are incorrect because they are not units of measurement.

193. **c.** A mouse is a type of rodent; an elm is a type of tree. Choices **a** and **b** are incorrect because a leaf and a trunk are parts of a tree, not types of trees. A squirrel (choice **d**) is not a rodent.

194. **b.** *Elated* is the opposite of *despondent; enlightened* is the opposite of *ignorant.*

195. **d.** A marathon is a long race and hibernation is a lengthy period of sleep. The answer is not choice **a** or **b** because even though a bear and winter are related to hibernation, neither of these completes the analogy. Choice **c** is incorrect because *sleep* and *dream* are not synonymous.

196. **a.** If someone has been humiliated, they have been greatly embarrassed. If someone is terrified, they are extremely frightened. The answer is not choice **b** because an agitated person is not necessarily frightened. Choices **c** and **d** are incorrect because neither word expresses a state of being frightened.

197. **d.** An odometer is an instrument used to measure mileage. A compass is an instrument used to determine direction. Choices **a, b,** and **c** are incorrect because none are instruments.

198. **a**. An optimist is a person whose outlook is cheerful. A pessimist is a person whose outlook is gloomy. The answer is not choice **b** because a pessimist does not have to be mean. Choices **c** and **d** are incorrect because neither of these adjectives describes the outlook of a pessimist.

199. **c**. A sponge is a porous material. Rubber is an elastic material. Choice **a** is incorrect because rubber would not generally be referred to as massive. The answer is not choice **b** because even though rubber is a solid, its most noticeable characteristic is its elasticity. Choice **d** is incorrect because rubber has flexibility.

200. **d.** *Candid* and *indirect* refer to opposing traits. *Honest* and *untruthful* refer to opposing traits. The answer is not choice **a,** because *frank* means the same thing as *candid. Wicked* (choice **b**) is incorrect because even though it refers to a negative trait, it does not mean the opposite of *honest.* Choice **c** is incorrect because *truthful* and *honest* mean the same thing.

201. **d.** A pen is a tool used by a poet. A needle is a tool used by a tailor. The answer is not choice **a, b,** or **c** because none are people and therefore cannot complete the analogy.

SET 13 (Page 29)

202. **d.** A can of paint is to a paint brush as a spool of thread is to a sewing needle. This is a relationship of function. Both show the tool needed to perform a task.

203. **a.** Grapes are to a pear as cheese is to butter. This relationship shows the grouping or category to which something belongs. Grapes and pears are fruit; cheese and butter are both dairy products.

204. **d.** An oar is to a canoe as a steering wheel is to a car. This is a functional relationship. The oar helps to steer the canoe in the way that the steering wheel steers the car.

205. **a.** Cup is to bowl as vacuum cleaner is to broom. This is another relationship about function. The cup and bowl are both used for eating. The vacuum cleaner and broom are both used for cleaning.

206. **d.** Sheep are to sweater as pine trees are to log cabin. Wool comes from the sheep to make a sweater; wood comes from the trees to make the log cabin.

207. **a.** Hand is to ring as head is to cap. A ring is worn on a person's hand; a cap is worn on a person's head.

208. **b.** A palm tree is to a pine tree as a bathing suit is to a parka. This relationship shows an opposite—warm to cold. Palm trees grow in warm climates and pine trees grow in cold climates. Bathing suits are worn in warm weather; parkas are worn in cold weather.

209. **d.** Batteries are to a flashlight as telephone wires are to a telephone. The batteries provide power to the flashlight; the wires send power to the telephone.

210. **d.** A fish is to a dragonfly as a chicken is to corn. Fish eat insects; chickens eat corn.

211. **a.** A telephone is to a stamped letter as an airplane is to a bus. A telephone and letter are both forms of communication. An airplane and bus are both forms of transportation.

212. **c.** A trapeze performer is to a clown as swings are to a sliding board. This relationship shows a classification. Trapeze performers and clowns are found at circuses; swings and sliding boards are found on playgrounds.

213. **c.** Camera is to photograph as tea kettle is to a cup of tea. The camera is used to make the photo; the tea kettle is used to make the tea.

214. **b.** Hat and mittens are to desert as snorkel and flippers are to snow. This relationship shows an opposition. The hat and mittens are **not** worn in the desert; the snorkel and flippers are **not** worn in the snow.

215. **d.** Car is to horse and buggy as computer is to pen and ink. This relationship shows the difference between modern times and times past.

216. **c.** Leather boots are to cow as pearl necklace is to oyster. The leather to make the boots comes from a cow; the pearls to make the necklace come from oysters.

217. **b.** A toddler is to an adult as a caterpillar is to a butterfly. This relationship shows the young and the adult. The caterpillar is an early stage of the adult butterfly.

218. **b.** Towel is to bathtub as chest of drawers is to bed. The towel and bathtub are both found in a bathroom; the chest and the bed are both found in a bedroom.

219. **a.** A snow-capped mountain is to a crocodile as a cactus is to a starfish. This relationship shows an opposition. The crocodile does **not** belong on the mountain; the starfish does **not** belong in the desert.

220. **c.** A shirt is to a button as a belt is to a belt buckle. A button is used to close a shirt; a belt buckle is used to close a belt.

221. **c.** A penny is to a dollar as a small house is to a skyscraper. This relationship shows smaller to larger. A penny is much smaller than a dollar; a house is much smaller than a skyscraper.

SET 14 (Page 35)

222. **b.** Guitar is to horn as hammer is to saw. This relationship is about grouping. The guitar and horn are musical instruments. The hammer and saw are carpentry tools.

223. **d.** Tree is to leaf as bird is to feather. This relationship shows part to whole. The leaf is a part of the tree; the feather is a part of the bird.

224. **c.** House is to tent as truck is to wagon. The house is a more sophisticated form of shelter than is the tent; the truck is a more sophisticated mode of transportation than is the wagon.

225. **c.** Scissors is to knife as pitcher is to watering can. This relationship is about function. The scissors and knife are both used for cutting. The pitcher and watering can are both used for watering.

226. **b.** A T-shirt is to a pair of shoes as a chest of drawers is to a couch. The relationship shows to which group something belongs. The T-shirt and shoes are both articles of clothing; the chest and couch are both pieces of furniture.

227. **d.** A bookshelf is to a book as a refrigerator is to a carton of milk. The book is placed on a bookshelf; the milk is placed in a refrigerator.

228. **d.** A squirrel is to an acorn as a bird is to a worm. A squirrel eats acorns; a bird eats worms.

229. **b.** An eye is to a pair of binoculars as a mouth is to a microphone. This relationship shows magnification. The binoculars help one to see farther. The microphone helps one to speak louder.

230. **a.** Knitting needles are to sweater as a computer is to a report. This relationship shows the tool needed to make a product. The knitting needles are used to create the sweater; the computer is used to write a report.

231. **b.** Bread is to knife as log is to ax. This relationship shows function. The knife cuts the bread; the ax chops the log.

232. **b.** Closet is to shirt as kitchen cabinets are to cans of food. The shirt is stored in the closet; the food is stored in the cabinets.

233. **a.** Pyramid is to triangle as cube is to square. This relationship shows dimension. The triangle shows one dimension of the pyramid; the square is one dimension of the cube.

234. **c.** Toothbrush is to toothpaste as butter knife is to butter. This relationship shows function. The toothbrush is used to apply the toothpaste to teeth; the knife is used to apply butter to bread.

235. **c.** Fly is to ant as snake is to lizard. The fly and ant are both insects; the snake and lizard are both reptiles.

236. **a.** Sail is to sailboat as pedal is to bicycle. The sail makes the sailboat move; the pedal makes the bicycle move.

237. **d.** Hose is to firefighter as needle is to nurse. This relationship shows the tools of the trade. A hose is a tool used by a firefighter; a needle is a tool used by a nurse.

238. **c.** A U.S. flag is to a fireworks display as a Halloween mask is to a pumpkin. This relationship shows symbols. The flag and fireworks are symbols for the Fourth of July. The mask and pumpkin are symbols of Halloween.

239. **d.** Newspaper is to book as trumpet is to banjo. The newspaper and book are to be read; the trumpet and banjo are musical instruments to be played.

240. **b.** Dishes are to kitchen sink as car is to hose. Dishes are cleaned in the sink; the car is cleaned with the hose.

241. **a.** The United States is to the world as a brick is to a brick house. This relationship shows part to whole. The United States is one part of the world; the brick is one part of the house.

SET 15 (Page 41)

242. **b.** The three above the line are all insects. The hamster and squirrel are rodents, so the correct choice is **b** because the mouse is also a rodent. The other three choices are not rodents.

243. **a.** In the relationship above the line, the ladder and hose are tools used by the firefighter. In the relationship below the line, the stethoscope and thermometer are tools used by the veterinarian.

244. **c.** A table made of wood could come from an oak tree. A shirt made of cloth could come from a cotton plant. Choice **a** looks like a reasonable answer if you apply the same sentence: "A shirt made of cloth could come from sewing." But this is not the same relationship as the one above the line. The oak and the cotton are both materials used to make the table and the shirt.

245. **d.** The words above the line show a continuum: *command* is more extreme than *rule*, and *dictate* is more extreme than *command*. Below the line the continuum is as follows: *sleep* is more than *doze,* and *hibernate* is more than *sleep*. The other choices are not related in the same way.

246. **a.** A banquet and a feast are both large meals; a palace and a mansion are both large places of shelter.

247. **b.** A fence and a wall mark a boundary. A path and an alley mark a passageway.

248. **c.** The objects above the line are all tools used by a carpenter. The tools below the line are all used by a gardener.

249. **b.** The relationship above the line is that snow on a mountain creates conditions for skiing. Below the line the relationship is that warmth at a lake creates conditions for swimming.

250. **d.** Above the line the relationship shows a progression of sources of light. The relationship below the line shows a progression of types of housing, from smallest to largest. Choice **a** is incorrect because a tent is smaller than a house. Choices **b** and **c** are wrong because they are not part of the progression.

251. **a.** The relationship above the line is as follows: aspirin is a medicine; medicine is sold in a pharmacy. Below the line, the relationship is: lettuce is a vegetable; vegetables are bought in a grocery.

252. **d.** The tadpole is a young frog; frogs are amphibians. The lamb is a young sheep; sheep are mammals. Animal (choice **a**) is incorrect because it is too large a grouping: animals include insects, birds, mammal, reptiles, and amphibians. Choices **b** and **c** are incorrect because they are not part of the progression.

253. **b.** Walk, skip, and run represent a continuum of movement: skipping is faster than walking; running is faster than skipping. Below the line, the continuum is about throwing. Pitch is faster than toss; hurl is faster than pitch.

254. **c.** The honeybee, angel, and bat all have wings; they are capable of flying. The kangaroo, rabbit, and grasshopper are all capable of hopping.

255. **a.** Above the line, the relationship is as follows: a daisy is a type of flower, and a flower is a type of plant. Below the line, the relationship is as follows: a bungalow is a type of house, and a house is a type of building.

SET 16 (Page 43)

256. **b.** A leaf is a part of a tree; a shelf is a part of a bookcase.

257. **d.** A key is a part of a piano; a brick is part of a wall.

258. **a.** A group of wolves is a pack; a group of lions is a pride.

259. **a.** A ruler measures length; a scale measures weight.

260. **d.** Broccoli is a kind of vegetable; Dalmatian is a kind of canine.

261. **e.** An oar propels a canoe; a foot propels a skateboard.

262. **c.** *Fray* and *ravel* are synonyms, as are *jolt* and *shake*.

263. **c.** An elephant is a pachyderm; a kangaroo is a marsupial.

264. **e.** *Depressed* is an intensification of *sad; exhausted* is an intensification of *tired.*

265. **a.** A psychologist treats a neurosis; an ophthalmologist treats a cataract.

266. **e.** A binding surrounds a book; a frame surrounds a picture.

267. **b.** One explores in order to discover; one researches in order to learn.

268. **c.** Upon harvesting, cotton is gathered into bales; grain is gathered into shocks.

269. **a.** *Division* and *section* are synonyms; *layer* and *tier* are synonyms.

270. **a.** *Pastoral* describes rural areas: *metropolitan* describes urban areas.

271. **d.** A mechanic works in a garage; a surgeon works in a hospital.

272. **c.** A chickadee is a type of bird; a Siamese is a type of cat.

273. **e.** To saunter is to walk slowly; to drizzle is to rain slowly.

274. **c.** A skein is a quantity of yarn; a ream is a quantity of paper.

275. **b.** To tailor a suit is to alter it; to edit a manuscript is to alter it.

SET 17 (Page 45)

276. **d.** A conductor leads an orchestra; a skipper leads a crew.

277. **a.** Jaundice is an indication of a liver problem; rash is an indication of a skin problem.

278. **b.** A cobbler makes and repairs shoes; a contractor builds and repairs buildings.

279. **e.** To be phobic is to be extremely fearful; to be asinine is to be extremely silly.

280. **c.** Obsession is a greater degree of interest; fantasy is a greater degree of dream.

281. **d.** Devotion is characteristic of a monk; wanderlust is characteristic of a rover.

282. **e.** Slapstick results in laughter; horror results in fear.

283. **b.** Verve and enthusiasm are synonyms; devotion and reverence are synonyms.

284. **c.** A cacophony is an unpleasant sound; a stench is an unpleasant smell.

285. **a.** A conviction results in incarceration; a reduction results in diminution.

286. **a.** The deltoid is a muscle; the radius is a bone.

287. **d.** *Umbrage* and *offense* are synonyms; *elation* and *jubilance* are synonyms.

288. **b.** Being erudite is a trait of a professor; being imaginative is a trait of an inventor.

289. **d.** *Dependable* and *capricious* are antonyms; *capable* and *inept* are antonyms.

290. **a.** A palm (tree) has fronds; a porcupine has quills.

291. **e.** A metaphor is a symbol; an analogy is a comparison.

292. **d.** A dirge is a song used at a funeral; a jingle is a song used in a commercial.

293. **e.** *Feral* and *tame* are antonyms; *ephemeral* and *immortal* are antonyms.

294. **a.** A spy acts in a clandestine manner; an accountant acts in a meticulous manner.

295. **c.** *Hegemony* means *dominance; autonomy* means *independence.*

296. **e.** An aerie is where an eagle lives; a house is where a person lives.

SET 18 (Page 47)

297. **a.** *Mele* means leather; *broon* means shoe; *blenc* means white, *kaal* means laces. Therefore, *blenckaal* means white laces.

298. **b.** *Lilo* means green; *bix* means soup; *lerno* means vegetable; *marj* means paint. Therefore, *lilolerno* means green vegetable.

299. **d.** From *yoologarn* and *yoologlink*, you can determine that *yoola* means red. Knowing this, you can determine that *glink* means wagon and *nara* means wheel. Therefore, *narapluh* is the only choice that could mean wheelbarrow.

300. **a.** *Jabber* means pronounce; *lota* is the same as the suffix -ment; *enna* is the same as the prefix mis-; *havre* means represent. Since the only word that has not been defined is *relm*, it is reasonable to conclude that *relmlota* is the only choice that could mean appointment.

301. **c.** In this language, the adjective follows the noun. From *dionot* and *blyonot*, you can determine that *onot* means oak. From *blyonot* and *blycrin*, you can determine that *bly* means leaf. Therefore, *crin* means maple. Because the adjective maple comes after the noun, *patricrin* is the only possible choice.

302. **c.** In this language the noun appears first and the adjectives follow. Since *agnos* means spider and should appear first, choices **a** and **d** can be ruled out. Choice **b** can be ruled out because *delano* means snake.

303. **a.** *Myn* means saddle; *cabel* means horse; *cono* means trail; and *wir* means ride. Therefore, *cabelwir* is the correct answer.

304. **c.** In this language, the adjective follows the noun. From *godabim* and *romzbim*, you can determine that *bim* means kidney. From *romzbim* and *romzbako*, you can determine that *romz* means beans. Therefore, *bako* means wax. Because the adjective wax must come after the noun in this language, *wasibako* is the only choice.

305. **b.** *Tam* means sky; *ceno* means blue; *rax* means cheese; *apl* means star; and *mitl* means bright. So *mitltam* means bright sky.

306. **d.** *Gorbl* means fan; *flur* means belt; *pixn* means ceiling; *arth* means tile; and *tusl* means roof. Therefore, *pixnarth* is the correct choice.

307. **d.** *Hapl* means cloud; *lesh* means burst; *srench* means pin; *och* means ball; and *resbo* means nine. *Leshsrench* (choice **a**) doesn't contain any of the words needed for cloud nine. We know that *och* means ball, so that rules out choices **c** and **d**. When you combine *hapl* (cloud) with *resbo* (nine), you get the correct answer.

308. **d.** *Migen* means cup; *lasan* means board; *poen* means walk; *cuop* means pull; and *dansa* means man. The only possible choices, then, are choices **a** and **d**. Choice **a** can be ruled out because *migen* means cup.

SET 19 (Page 50)

309. **c.** *Spasir* means dog; *quot* means house; *tor* means sheep; *lann* means skin. Choice **c** is the only possible option.

310. **b.** According to this language, *faur* means bring. The suffix -ing is represented by -*y*. Since choice **b** is the only one that ends in the letter *y*, this is the only possible option.

311. **b.** *Bose* means the root word *mili-*; the suffix -*amint* means the same as the English suffix -*tant*; the root word *insic-* means habit; *boca* means the suffix -*ual* of *habitual*; and -*amene* means the suffix -*able*. (Because *insica* means habit, choices **a**, **c**, and **d** can easily be ruled out.)

312. **a.** *Erane* means ship; *acal* means shape; *arap* means relation; and *alon* means mate. *Arap* means relation, so that rules out choices **b** and **d.** *Acal* means shape, so that rules out choice **c.** That leaves choice **a** as the only possible answer.

313. **d.** *Shillen* means time; *acen* means table; *ablot* means cloth; *mica* means ground; and *erran* means water. Therefore, *erranacen* means water table.

314. **b.** *Jusl* means obstacle; *lagen* means course; *namer* means work; *osto* means college; and *fifer* means life. Because *namer* means work, it must be present in the answer, so that rules out choice **c.** In choice **a**, *jusl* means obstacle, so choice **a** is not the answer. In choice **d**, *osto* means college, so choice **d** cannot be the answer. That leaves choice **b** as the only possible answer.

315. **a.** *Hamo* means last; *mone* means minute; *moze* means word; *halli* means good; *gun* means the suffix -ness. The only choice that uses the suffix is choice **a.**

316. **d.** *Affon* means straw; *goml* means hat; *nagl* means berry; and *afton* means "rasp" in raspberry. In the word hatband, "hat" requires the word *goml.* That rules out choices **a** and **c.** *Afton* in choice **b** means "rasp," so that rules out choice **b.** That leaves choice **d** the only possible choice.

317. **a.** *Gero* means false, *mea* means pretense, *gene* means clock, *omo* means radio, and *gim* means alarm. Thus, *gerogim* is the correct choice.

318. **d.** *Asta* means stuffed; *ose* means chair; *esta* means leather; *costa* means lift; and *fut* means off. Thus, *osecosta* means chair lift.

319. **c.** In this language, the root word *maga*, which means power, follows the affix (*dwil, o-,* or *fer-*). Therefore, in the word overpower, the root word and the affix are reversed in the artificial language. The only choice, then, is *magazen*, because *magafer* would mean less power.

320. **a.** *Haga* means apple; *upl* means pie; *port* means juice; *hogga* means grape; and *grop* means jelly. Thus, *hoggaport* means grape juice.

SET 20 (Page 53)

321. b. Jim broke into a vehicle without permission from the owner and stole a purse out of the vehicle.

322. a. Ernie threatened to harm Harold by breaking his legs if Harold reports a crime—his nose being broken—to the police.

323. d. This is the only situation where notice has been given that no one is allowed on the property. No one can be arrested for trespassing for being in their own residence (choice **a**). Answer **b** is wrong because no verbal or written notice to stay off the property has been given. Answer **c** is wrong because Frank left the dealership once he knew he wasn't allowed to be there.

324. d. Emilio is on city property (the street) and a stranger asks him for money.

325. c. Fred intentionally damaged another person's car without the owner's permission. The actions in answers **a** and **d** are unintentional, and the person in answer **b** is damaging his own property.

326. b. Ed lied to a peace officer by filing a report with police, knowing that the statement he gave to police about his car being stolen was material to the investigation.

327. c. Sandra is the only one actually operating a vehicle on a public street while intoxicated.

328. b. Rudy threatens to bash out the headlights on Edward's car, thereby threatening to damage another person's property. In the other options, there is no threat or apparent attempt to annoy, alarm, or torment anyone. The landlord in **d** is within his rights because the tenant is behind on her rent.

329. a. Greg possesses what he wants others to believe is a bomb and is using it in a manner calculated to cause alarm. In option **b**, all we know is that Stuart hears ticking noises coming from a package. There isn't enough information to be able to assume that the package contains a hoax bomb, and there is no presumption of possession on Stuart's part simply because he picked up the package. In choices **c** and **d**, there is no apparent attempt to pass off the objects in question as bombs.

330. c. Edith is trying to defraud the antique dealer by claiming that she owns an original by a famous poet. In option **a**, there is nothing to indicate that Bess altered any item or that she intended to defraud or harm anyone. She is not likely to expect anyone to believe that she is the Betsy Ross who created the first American flag. The same logic applies to option **b**. In option **d**, Wendell has not tried to alter an object to increase its value, nor has he tried to defraud or harm anyone.

331. d. Leo is guilty of stealing his new stereo because he wrote a check on an account he knew no longer existed. In both options **a** and **b**, the writers of the bad checks "made good" on the checks, in the case of **a** by way of an overdraft agreement with the bank. In **c**, even though Jacob closed his account, he has left enough money in the account to pay the outstanding check.

332. **b.** Vinnie's cymbal concert is clearly designed to disrupt the meeting. The other options provide no serious obstruction or interference.

333. **d.** Brent clearly intends to burn his landlord's vehicle. The other options provide examples of people who may be careless but have no intent to cause harm.

334. **a.** Alan and Terrence are in a public place and are fighting. In choice **b,** the couple is arguing, not fighting. In choice **c,** the men are not in public. In choice **d,** there are only two incidents of physical contact—not enough to constitute a "fight."

SET 21 (Page 59)

335. **a.** A truck with the motor running backed up to the rear door of a closed business at 2 a.m. is suspicious. Delivery vans owned by businesses are commonly parked on store property after hours (choice **c**). Window shoppers, whether elderly (choice **b**) or teenaged (choice **d**), aren't as likely to be burglars as the scene detailed in answer **a**.

336. **c.** The officer is looking for a suspect dressed in dark clothing who has been seen walking up and down a residential street during a specific time span—a window peeper. The other answers suggest normal neighborhood activity, but there is no "normal" explanation for what the man in answer **c** is doing.

337. **b.** Seeing a teenager with a spray paint can is the most suspicious of the incidents described since Officer Yang is looking for graffiti artists. Spray paint is not an item most people carry around with them and is suspicious given the circumstances.

338. **d.** Seeing a man running through the vacant lot with a bulky item under his shirt should make the officer suspicious. A purse snatcher would very likely choose to run through the vacant lot to get away from the area and would very likely want to hide an object as obvious as a woman's purse from view. Option **a** is not particularly suspicious given that most car alarms activate the car horn and car alarms frequently go off in parking lots. In option **b**, a car with all tires on flat may indicate criminal mischief but isn't linked to the purse snatchings. In option **c**, a woman's voice raised in anger would be a plausible thing to hear following a purse snatching, but it's not nearly as suspicious as the situation in answer **d**.

339. **b.** A panel truck pulling out of a vacant lot near a car dealership suffering from a rash of theft of auto parts is suspicious. The truck would be able to hold plenty of auto parts. The two rollerbladers in choice **c** aren't likely to be able to carry off a new van running board without attracting some attention. The man in his early twenties in choice **a** appears to be doing what a lot of people do late at night, which is look at new cars without having to worry about sales personnel. And it is not unusual for cleanup crews to arrive late at night after everyone has gone, as in option **d**.

340. **c.** The odd behavior and the location of the two figures should cause the officer to investigate, given the problems the school has been having.

341. **a.** The witnesses seem to agree that the plate starts out with the letter J. Three witnesses agree that the plate ends with 12L. Three witnesses think that the second letter is X, and a different three think that the third letter is K. The plate description that has all of these common elements is answer **a**.

342. **a.** Three of the witness agree that the first number is 9. Three agree that the second number is 2. Three witnesses agree that the third number is 6; three others agree that the fourth number is also 6. Answer **a** is the best choice because it is made up of the numbers that most of the witnesses agree that they saw.

343. **d.** Step 2 says the officer should have asked the security guard to fill out a witness statement and a complaint form.

344. **c.** Step 5 of the procedures for arrest and transport specifies that the prisoner should be transported directly to the jail. Officer DeVero should not have stopped the woman who ran a stop sign.

345. **b.** The suspect described in Theft #3 does not match Alfonso's suspect description very closely. The women in 1, 2, and 4 all appear to be the same woman Alfonso saw because of the similarities in height, weight, hair, and eyewear.

346. **c.** The suspect described in Robbery #2 has a crew-cut hair style, is at least five inches taller than the other suspects, and is about 60 pounds heavier. The other three descriptions are much more likely to be of the same man because they all describe a similar build and mention one earring or a pierced ear.

SET 22 (Page 65)

347. **c.** Since Erin's parents think a dog would not be happy in an apartment, we can reasonably conclude that the family lives in an apartment. We do not know if Erin's parents dislike dogs (choice **a**), or if Erin dislikes birds (choice **b**). There is no support for choice **d**.

348. **d.** It is reasonable to conclude that Mike likes singing and dancing because he looks forward to doing these things at music camp. There is no information that supports any of the other three choices.

349. **c.** Given the information presented, the only statement that could be considered true is that the fruit should not be eaten because it is poisonous. There is no support that taxol is poisonous or that taxol has cured anyone (choices **a** and **b**). Neither is there support for choice **d**.

350. **a.** Because Mr. Sanchez spends many hours during the weekend working in his vegetable garden, it is reasonable to suggest that he enjoys this work. There is no information to suggest that he does not like classical music. Although Mrs. Sanchez likes to cook, there is nothing that indicates she cooks vegetables (choice **c**). Mrs. Sanchez likes to read, but there is no information regarding the types of books she reads (choice **d**).

351. **b.** Since the two inches of snow was an 102-year-old record, choice **b** is true. Choice **a** cannot be verified because the temperature may have reached 4 degrees prior to 1896. There is no clear support for choices **c** and **d**.

352. **d.** The first sentence and last sentence make this statement true. There is no support for choice **a**. There is no indication that the train is cheaper (choice **b**). The roundtrip tickets make choice **c** untrue.

353. **b.** Since the seahorse populations have declined as a result of fishing, their populations will increase if seahorse fishing is banned. There is no support for any of the other choices.

354. **a.** The fact that Vincent and Thomas live on the same street indicates that they live in the same neighborhood. There is no support for any of the other choices.

355. **d.** If Georgia is older than Marsha and Bart is older than Georgia, then Marsha has to be the youngest of the three. Choice **b** is clearly wrong because Bart is the oldest. There is no information in the paragraph to support either choice **a** or choice **c**.

356. **c.** If there were seven shows left, and five were sitcoms, this means that only two of the shows could possibly be dramas. Choices **a** and **b** may be true, but there is no evidence to indicate this as fact. The fact that all of the sitcoms remained does not necessarily mean that viewers prefer sitcoms (choice **d**).

357. **c.** Since the paragraph states that Marlee is the younger cousin, Sara must be older than Marlee. There is no information to support the other choices.

SET 23 (Page 68)

358. **b.** Because the first two statements are true, Wendell is the shortest of the three, so the third statement is false.

359. **c.** Because the first two statements are true, both Zoe and Heather read more books than Jane, but it is uncertain as to whether Zoe read more books than Heather.

360. **c.** The first two statements give information about Joshua's white socks and blue socks. Information about socks of any other color cannot be determined.

361. **a.** Because the first two statements are true, pistachios are the most expensive of the three.

362. **a.** If no shingles are purple and all of the houses have roofs with shingles, none of the houses has a purple roof.

363. **b.** From the first two statements we know that of the three cities, City A has the highest population, so the third statement must be false.

364. **a.** According to the first two statements, Paws weighs the most and Tabby weighs the least.

365. **c.** Although all of Harriet's succulents are flowering plants, it cannot be determined by the information given whether or not all succulents are flowering plants.

366. **a.** Since the Hide-Away costs more than the Cozy Inn, and the Hotel Victoria costs more than the Hide-Away, it is true that the Hotel Victoria costs the most.

367. **a.** From the first two statements, you know that Troop 101 sold the most cookies, so Troop 101 would have sold more than Troop 103.

368. **b.** We know from the first two statements that James jumps highest. Therefore, the third statement must be false.

SET 24 (Page 70)

369. a. From the first statement, we know that bran cereal has more fiber than both oat cereal and corn cereal. From the second statement we know that rice cereal has less fiber than both corn and wheat cereals. Therefore, rice cereal has the least amount of fiber.

370. c. We only know that Jasmine weighs more than Jason. There is no way to tell whether Jasmine also weighs more than Jenna.

371. c. We know from the first two statements that Tuesday had the highest temperature, but we cannot know whether Monday's temperature was higher than Tuesday's.

372. b. Spot is bigger than King, and Ralph is bigger than Spot. Therefore, King must be smaller than Ralph.

373. a. There are fewer oranges than either apples or lemons, so the statement is true.

374. b. Because the first two statements are true, Rebecca's house is also northeast of the Shop and Save Grocery, which means that the third statement is false.

375. a. Joe is younger than Kathy and older than Mark, so Mark must be younger than Kathy.

376. c. We know only that long-tailed Gangles have spots. We cannot know for certain if long-tailed Gangles also have short hair.

377. c. The first two statements indicate that Battery Y lasts the least amount of time, but it cannot be determined if Battery Z lasts longer than Battery X.

378. b. Given the information in the first two statements, Bryant is sitting in front of both Jerome and Martina, so the third statement must be false.

379. b. Because the first two statements are true, Penfield is west of Centerville and southwest of Middletown. Therefore, the third statement is false.

SET 25 (Page 72)

380. **c.** Both the car and the train are quicker than the bus, but there is no way to make a comparison between the train and the car.

381. **a.** We know that there are Signots with buttons, or Lamels, and that there are yellow Signots, which have no buttons. Therefore, Lamels do not have buttons and cannot be yellow.

382. **a.** The market is one block west of the hotel. The drugstore is two blocks west of the hotel, so the drugstore is west of the market.

383. **c.** There is not enough information to verify the third statement.

384. **b.** Rulers are the most expensive item.

385. **b.** The first two statements indicate there are more yellow jelly beans than red and green.

386. **c.** Cloudy days are the most windy, but there is not enough information to compare the wind on the foggy days with the wind on the sunny days.

387. **a.** Of the three, the drugstore has the best selection of postcards.

388. **b.** This is the order of the cars from left to right: minivan, pickup, sedan, sport utility vehicle.

389. **a.** To the extent that a toothpick is useful, it has value.

SET 26 (Page 74)

390. **a.** Since one-half of the four children are girls, two must be boys. It is not clear which children have blue or brown eyes.

391. **d.** All baseball caps have brims, since baseball caps are hats (Fact 3) and all hats have brims (Fact 1). This rules out Statement III—but it doesn't follow that all caps, a category that may include caps that are not baseball caps, have brims (Statement I). Statement II cannot be confirmed, either, since it is possible, given the information, that all baseball caps are black.

392. **b.** The first statement cannot be true because only female birds lay eggs. Statement II is true because hens are chickens and chickens are birds. Statement III is also true because if only some chickens are hens, then some must not be hens.

393. **d.** None of the three statements is supported by the known facts.

394. **c.** Statements I and II are not supported by the facts. Statement III is true because if all storybooks have pictures and only some have words, then some storybooks have both words and pictures.

395. **d.** There is not enough information to support any of the statements. Robert is known to have a minvan, but it is not known which of his vehicles is red. Robert may have a pickup or sport utility vehicle, so the second statement cannot be supported. There is no way to know what Robert's favorite color is (statement III).

396. **a.** Since Maui is an island and islands are surrounded by water, Maui must be surrounded by water. There is not enough information to support statements II and III.

397. **c.** If all drink mixes are beverages and some beverages are red, then some drink mixes are red (statement I). Since all beverages are drinkable and all drink mixes are beverages, then all red drink mixes must be drinkable (statement III). Statement II can be ruled out.

398. **d.** There is no information in the facts to support statements I or II. Statement III is clearly wrong because, according to Fact 1, no frames cost less than $35.

399. **b.** Since some pens don't write, some writing utensils don't write (statement I). Since there are blue pens and since pens are writing utensils, some writing utensils are blue (statement II). There is not enough information to support statement III.

400. **c.** If Mary always tells the truth, then both Ann and Mary have cats (statements I and II), and Ann is lying (statement III).

401. **b.** Statement II is the only true statement. Since all dogs like to run, then the ones who like to swim also like to run. There is no support for statement I or statement III.

SET 27 (Page 78)

402. **d.** After all the switches were made, Reinhart is directly behind the vehicle, Baker is on the driver's side of the vehicle, Lopez is on the passenger side, and O'Malley is behind Reinhart.

403. **b.** Nurse Kemp has worked more shifts in a row than Nurse Calvin; therefore, Kemp has worked more than eight shifts. The number of Kemp's shifts plus the number of Rogers' shifts (five) cannot equal fifteen or more, the number of Miller's shifts. Therefore, Kemp has worked nine shifts in a row (5 + 9 = 14).

404. **c.** If Randy is two months older than Greg, then Ned is three months older than Greg and one month older than Randy. Kent is younger than both Randy and Ned. Ned is the oldest.

405. **c.** After all the switches were made, Officer Sheen is in front of the house. Officer Roth is in the alley behind the house; Officer Michaels is on the north side, Officer Jensen on the south.

406. **d.** After all the switches were made, Mr. Kirk worked on Tuesday. Mr. Carter worked on Monday, Ms. Johnson on Wednesday, and Ms. Falk on Thursday.

407. **a.** Mr. Temple has the most seniority, but he does not want the job. Next in line is Mr. Rhodes, who has more seniority than Ms. West or Ms. Brody.

408. **b.** Tall, thin, and middle-aged are the elements of the description repeated most often and are therefore the most likely to be accurate.

409. **b.** Bush committed the most serious offense, described as a more serious crime than James, who is the only person described as having been arrested for a felony, and Bush has also served the most time of any of the prisoners.

410. **c.** After all the switching was done, Jenkins was directly behind the receiver. Calvin and Burton had fallen. Zeller remained in the rear.

411. **d.** Sexton is farther away than Fromme, who is five miles away, and closer than Smith, who is seven miles away.

412. **a.** Baxter should be assigned to study with Carter. Baxter cannot be assigned with Adam, because they have already been together for seven class periods. If Baxter is assigned to work with Dennis, that would leave Adam with Carter, but Carter does not want to work with Adam.

413. **a.** If George is sitting at Henry's left, George's seat is 252. The next seat to the left, then, is 251.

SET 28 (Page 81)

414. **d.** The total of the three programs (2 million + 0.5 million + 3 million) is 5.5 million. That leaves 1.5 million (7 million – 5.5 million), and the only single program needing that amount is senate office building remodeling.

415. **b.** The only two programs that total 1.5 million dollars are harbor improvements and school music program.

416. **a.** The total cost of the school music program and national radio is 1 million dollars, the amount left after the international airport and agricultural subsidies are funded.

417. **c.** J will only work in episodes in which M is working and there are no restrictions on O's schedule. However, N will not work with K, so M must appear and O may appear.

418. **d.** K will not work with N, so choices **c** and **e** are incorrect. M can only work every other week, so choice **a** is incorrect. Since M is not working, J will not work, so choice **b** is incorrect.

419. **b.** Only choice **b** contains no more than two R-rated movies (*Shout* and *Mist*), at least one G and one PG (*Fly*, *Abra Cadabra*, and *Jealousy*), and only one foreign film (*Mist*).

420. **c.** The first showing of *Trek* will be over at 10:00. Then, the employees will need 20 minutes to clean the theater, which is 10:20. Since the movies always start on the quarter hour, the second showing of *Trek* will be 10:30.

421. **e.** Since *Shout* is doing the most business and *Trek* the second most, they should remain in the two largest theaters. Also, the theater never shows a foreign film in the largest theater. Theaters 3 and 4 must show the movies that are rated G and PG, so the movies that are there must stay there. The most logical choice is to put *Mist* in Theater 5 and *Fly* in Theater 6.

422. **a.** "Honey" and "Sittin' on the Dock of the Bay" are either 3 and 4 or 4 and 3. The Rascals appear on the list right after Otis Redding, who cannot be #3 (or he would be followed by Bobby Goldsboro), so "Honey" is #3, and "Sittin' on the Dock of the Bay" is #4; therefore choices **c** and **e** are incorrect. The Rascals are #5 (because they are right after Otis Redding), and Cream appears right after them, so choice **d** is incorrect. Since Cream has song #6, it cannot be "Hey Jude," so choice **b** is incorrect.

423. **d.** In the previous question, it was determined that #3 is "Honey," #4 is "Sittin' on the Dock of the Bay," #5 is "People Got to be Free," and #6 is "Sunshine of Your Love". Since the #1 song is not "Love Is Blue," #1 is "Hey Jude" and #2 is "Love Is Blue."

SET 29 (Page 86)

Here's a quick illustration of how to work "logic game" puzzles, using the situation in questions 424 and 425 as an example.

First, read the paragraph. Then construct a diagram or table like the one below. Write down the letters that represent the names of the people at the party. Next, add any other information that is given. You know that Quentin is an accountant and Sarah is a florist; you know which objects represent their type of work. You also know that Thomas is dressed as a camera, so he must be the photographer.

Q	accountant	pencil
R		
S	florist	flower
T	photographer	camera
U		

Since none of the men is a doctor, Rachel must be the doctor. That leaves Ulysses, who must be the chef. Once you've filled in your diagram and made the deductions, answering the questions is the easy part.

Q	accountant	pencil
R	doctor	thermometer
S	florist	flower
T	photographer	camera
U	chef	spoon

424. b. See the table above. The thermometer costume logically would be worn by the doctor. According to the information, none of the men is a doctor. Also, Sarah is a florist, so Rachel must be the doctor wearing the thermometer costume.

425. e. Ulysses cannot be a doctor, because that is Rachel. Quentin is an accountant, Thomas must be a photographer, and Sarah is a florist. That leaves chef for Ulysses. We also know the chef must be a man, because neither of the women is dressed as a spoon.

426. d. The person who ordered the vegetable burger cannot be sitting in spaces 1 or 6, because she is sitting between two people. She also cannot be sitting in spaces 3 or 4, because those customers did not order sandwiches. Since she is not sitting in space 2, she must be in space 5.

427. c. The customer who ordered soup must be in chair 3 or 4, where the non-sandwich orders go. The other non-sandwich order is fried eggs, and that person is sitting next to the customer in chair 5 (who ordered the vegetable burger), so the fried eggs go to chair 4 and the soup to chair 3.

428. b. The orders that go to chairs 3, 4, 5, and 6 are already determined, so the ham sandwich must go to chair 1 or 2. The customer who ordered the hamburger is not sitting next to the person who ordered the soup in chair 3, so the hamburger must go to chair 1 and the ham sandwich to chair 2.

429. a. The person who ordered potato salad cannot be in chair 1 or 6, since he is sitting between two people. The person who ordered fried eggs ordered hash browns and is sitting in chair 4. The person who ordered potato salad is on one side of chair 4, either 3 or 5. He cannot be in chair 5 and still be next to both the hash browns and the cole slaw, so he must be in chair 3, which is where the soup was ordered.

430. c. If the potato salad is with the soup and the hash browns are with the fried eggs, then the cole slaw must be with the ham sandwich, in chairs 2, 3, and 4. The lettuce salad is with the vegetable burger in chair 5. The onion rings belong to the cheeseburger in chair 6, leaving the french fries for the hamburger in chair 1.

431. **a.** The vice president's car cannot be red, because that is the CEO's car, which is in the first space. Nor can it be purple, because that is the treasurer's car, which is in the last space, or yellow, because that is the secretary's. The president's car must be blue, because it is parked between a red car (in the first space) and a green car, which must be the vice president's.

432. **c.** The CEO drives a red car and parks in the first space. Enid drives a green car; Bert's car is not in the first space; David's is not in the first space, but the last. Alice's car is parked next to David's, so Cheryl is the CEO.

433. **e.** Cheryl cannot be the secretary, since she's the CEO, nor can Enid, because she drives a green car, and the secretary drives a yellow car. David's, the purple car, is in the last space. Alice is the secretary, because her car is parked next to David's, which is where the secretary's car is parked.

SET 30 (Page 89)

434. d. The Whippets cannot be in Jersey, Hudson, or Fulton, since they have beaten those teams. The Antelopes are in Groton, so the Whippets are in Ivy.

435. e. The Panthers cannot be in Ivy or Groton, because the Whippets and Antelopes are there. Fulton has beaten the Panthers, so they cannot be in Fulton. Fulton has also beaten the Kangaroos, so the only town left for the Kangaroos is Jersey. That leaves Hudson for the Panthers.

436. b. Every team and town is matched up, except Fulton and the Gazelles, so the Gazelles must be in Fulton.

437. a. Kevin is allergic to daisies and iris; he's not getting gladioli because it's not his housewarming. The roses are going to Jenny, leaving the carnations for Kevin.

438. d. Jenny is getting roses and Kevin is getting carnations. Neither Liz nor Inez would be getting a housewarming present. Michael is getting gladioli.

439. e. The only flowers unassigned are iris and daisies. Liz is allergic to daisies, so she is getting the iris.

440. e. The city that got the least rain is in the desert. New Town is in the mountains. Last Stand got more rain than Olliopolis, so it cannot be the city with the least rain; also, Mile City cannot be the city with the least rain. Olliopolis got 44 inches of rain. Therefore, Polberg is in the desert and got 12 inches of rain.

441. a. Olliopolis got 44 inches of rain. Last Stand got more rain than that, so it got 65 inches, which is the most.

442. b. Olliopolis got 44 inches of rain, Last Stand got 65, and Polberg got 12. New Town is in the mountains, and the city in the mountains got 32 inches of rain. Therefore, Mile City got 27.

443. c. Olliopolis got 44 inches of rain, so it is not in the desert or the forest. The city in the mountains got 32 inches of rain; the coast 27. Therefore, Olliopolis is in a valley.

SET 31 (Page 92)

444. **d.** The moderator sits in seat #3. It cannot, then, be Gary or Jarrod or Lane, who sit next to the moderator. Heloise is not the moderator; therefore, the moderator is Kate.

445. **a.** Jarrod cannot sit in seat #3 because he is not the moderator. Nor can he sit in seat #2 or #4, because he does not sit next to the moderator. Heloise cannot sit on an end, nor in seat #3 or #4, so she is in seat #2, between the moderator (Kate) and Jarrod, who must be in seat #1.

446. **e.** Jarrod sits in seat #1 and is not the moderator; nor is he the pilot or the attorney. The attorney sits in seat #4, and cannot sit next to the explorer. Therefore, the pilot, Lane, is in seat #5, and the explorer must be in seat #1, Jarrod's seat.

447. **b.** Jarrod is the explorer, Lane is the pilot, Kate is the moderator, and Gary is the attorney. Heloise must be the writer.

448. **d.** Zinnia plants tomatoes each year, so choice **e** is incorrect. Each year she plants either carrots or cabbage, but not both. She will plant cabbage in the second year, so she will plant carrots in the first. She never plants carrots and peppers together, so the first year is tomatoes, carrots, beans and the second is tomatoes, cabbage, peppers.

449. **c.** Dusting must be done on Tuesday, Wednesday, or Thursday. However, the mopping is done on Thursday, and Terry does his task on Wednesday. Therefore, Sally does the dusting on Tuesday.

450. **d.** Terry does not dust, mop, do laundry, or vacuum. Therefore, Terry does the sweeping on Wednesday.

451. **b.** Dusting is on Tuesday, sweeping is on Wednesday, mopping is on Thursday, and laundry is on Friday. Therefore, the vacuuming is done on Monday.

452. **e.** Vernon does not vacuum, dust, or sweep. Randy does the vacuuming, Sally does the dusting, Terry does the sweeping—leaving laundry and mopping for Uma and Vernon. Uma does not do laundry; therefore, she must mop, and Vernon does the laundry.

453. **d.** Uma does the mopping, which is done on Thursday.

SET 32 (Page 95)

454. **d.** By stating that fitness walking does not require a commute to a health club, the author stresses the convenience of this form of exercise. The paragraph also states that fitness walking will result in a good workout. Choice **a** is incorrect because no comparison to weight lifting is made. Choice **b** may seem like a logical answer, but the paragraph only refers to people who are fitness walkers, so for others, a health club might be a good investment. Choice **c** is not in the passage. Although choice **e** seems logical, the paragraph does not indicate that the wrong shoes will produce major injuries.

455. **e.** This answer is implied by the statement that redistribution is needed so that people in emerging nations can have proper medical care. Choices **a, b,** and **c** are not mentioned in the passage. Choice **d** is also incorrect—the passage indicates that the distribution of medicine, not its production, is inadequate.

456. **b.** This answer is clearly stated in the first sentence of the paragraph. There is no support in the passage for choices **a, d,** or **e.** As for choice **c,** although mediation is mentioned, the statement does not indicate that victims should be the mediators.

457. **c.** This choice is supported as the best answer because the paragraph indicates that legislators once feared suggesting gas taxes, but now many of them are pushing bills in favor of these taxes. There is no indication that choice **a** is true. Choice **b** is wrong because the paragraph doesn't say why more gas taxes are being proposed. There is no support for choice **d.** Although choice **e** might be an attractive choice, the paragraph indicates that gas taxes are no longer political poison.

458. **a.** The paragraph clearly states that there are two differing opinions with regard to the use of calculators in the classroom. Although some people may believe that choice **b** is true, the paragraph does not indicate this. Choice **c** has no relation to the paragraph. Choice **d** makes logical sense, but the paragraph says nothing about cost. Choice **e** is an opinion that is not given in the paragraph.

459. **e.** This is clearly the best answer because the paragraph directly states that warm weather affects consumers' inclination to spend. It furthers states that the sales of single-family homes was at an all-time high. There is no support for choices **a** or **c.** Choice **b** is wrong because even though there were high sales for a particular February, this does not mean that sales are not higher in other months. Choice **d** presents a misleading figure of 4 million. The paragraph states that the record of 4.75 million was at an annual, not a monthly, rate.

460. **b.** The last sentence in the paragraph clearly gives support for the idea that the interest in Shakespeare is due to the development of his characters. Choice **a** is incorrect because the writer never makes this type of comparison. Choice **c** is wrong because even though scholars are mentioned in the paragraph, there is no indication that the scholars are compiling the anthology. Choice **d** is wrong because there is no support to show that most New Yorkers are interested in this work. There is no support for choice **e** either.

461. **c.** A change in employee social values over the past ten years is implied in the whole paragraph, but particularly in the first sentence. Choice **a** is incorrect because the loyalty of the managers to their corporations is never discussed. There is no support for choice **b.** In choice **d,** perhaps career advancement is less important than it once was, but the paragraph does not indicate that advancement is unimportant to managers. Choice **e** is an opinion that is not supported.

462. **b.** The support for choice **b** is given in the second sentence of the paragraph. Generation Xers like to work independently, which means they are self-directed. No support is given for either choice **a** or choice **c.** Choice **d** is not related to the paragraph. Although the paragraph mentions that Generation Xers like to be challenged, it does not say they like to challenge their bosses' attitudes; therefore, choice **e** can be ruled out.

463. **e.** The support for choice **e** is in the second sentence: ". . . we should make voting compulsory." Choice **a** has no relation to the paragraph. Although payment of taxes is mentioned in the paragraph, there is no support for the opinion expressed in choice **c.** Although the U.S. has low voter turnout, there is no support for the idea that most democracies have the same problem (choice **d**).

SET 33 (Page 98)

464. **d.** This answer is implied by the whole paragraph. The author stresses the need to read critically by performing thoughtful and careful operations on the text. Choice **a** is incorrect because the author never says that reading is dull. Choices **b**, **c**, and **e** are not supported by the paragraph.

465. **a.** The support for this choice is in the second sentence, which states that in some countries toxic insecticides are still legal. Choice **b** is incorrect because even though polar regions are mentioned in the paragraph, there is no support for the idea that warmer regions are not just as affected. There is no support for choice **c**. Choice **d** can be ruled out because there is nothing to indicate that DDT and toxaphene are the *most* toxic. Choice **e** is illogical.

466. **a.** The second and third sentence combine to give support to choice **a**. The statement stresses that there must be a judge's approval (i.e., legal authorization) before a search can be conducted. Choices **b** and **d** are wrong because it is not enough for the police to have direct evidence or a reasonable belief—a judge must authorize the search for it to be legal. Choices **c** and **e** are not mentioned in the passage.

467. **e.** The paragraph focuses on the idea that the jury system is different from what it was in colonial times. There is no support given for choices **a**, **b**, or **c**. Choice **d** is incorrect because, even though jurors in colonial times were expected to investigate and ask questions, this does not necessarily mean that they were more informed than today's jurors.

468. **e.** This answer is clearly stated in the last sentence of the paragraph. Choice **a** can be ruled out because there is no support to show that studying math is dangerous. Words are not mentioned in the passage, which rules out choice **b**. Choice **d** is a contradiction to the information in the passage. There is no support for choice **c**.

469. **d.** The last sentence states that new technologies are reported daily, and this implies that new technologies are being constantly developed. There is no support for choice **a**. With regard to choice **b**, stone tools were first used two and a half million years ago, but they were not necessarily in use all that time. Choice **c** is clearly wrong since the paragraph states when stone tools first came into use. Although some may agree that choice **e** is true, the author of the paragraph does not give support for this opinion.

470. **a.** The support for this choice is in the first two sentences, which state that scientists have made progress in the study of human development by studying mice and other creatures. Choice **b** can be ruled out with a careful reading. There is no support in the paragraph to indicate that scientists have learned to control human development; rather, they have learned about the mechanisms that control development. There is no support for choice **c** in the paragraph. Choices **d** and **e** can be ruled out because the paragraph states that scientists have made significant progress during the past five years, but it does not state that their progress and their interest began only five years ago.

471. **b.** This answer is clearly supported in the second sentence. Nothing in the paragraph suggests that it is a crime not to give a Miranda warning, so choice **a** is incorrect. Choice **c** is also wrong because police may interrogate as long as a warning is given. There is no support given for either choice **d** or **e**.

472. **c.** The last two sentences give direct support for this response. Choice **a** is somewhat of a contradiction because the author believes that librarians are trying to respond to the needs of readers. Choice **b** is attractive but is not in the passage. There is no indication that librarians have increased the popularity of CD-ROM and the Internet (choice **d**). Choice **e** is not in the passage.

473. **b.** The second sentence points out that goals and needs should be established before a company purchases a new technology such as videoconferencing. Choice **a** is incorrect because the paragraph indicates that videoconferencing is happening now; it is not necessarily the wave of the future. Choices **c**, **d**, and **e** are incorrect because neither of these is mentioned in the paragraph.

SET 34 (Page 102)

474. **d.** The final sentence of the paragraph supports choice **d.** The other choices are not in the passage. Choice **e** may seem attractive at first, but the paragraph says that e-mail should be concise and limited to one topic; it does not say that topic must be minor.

475. **d.** The author of this statement suggests that doctors are less independent. The author stresses that many doctors have lost authority. There is no support for the opinion that doctors resent the health-care managers, however—which rules out choice **a.** The doctors' training is never mentioned (choice **b**). Doctors may care about their patients (choice **c**), but this information is not part of the paragraph. Choice **e** is not mentioned.

476. **e.** The second sentence states that threading a needle involves motor skill. The other choices are not in the paragraph.

477. **a.** The paragraph states that Mars once had a thick atmosphere but that it was stripped away. The other choices, true or not, cannot be found in the passage.

478. **a.** The last sentence provides direct support for choice **a.** The author never suggests that any trees should be cut down or thinned out, which eliminates choices **b** and **c.** Choice **d** contradicts the author's opinion. The author suggests that old growth forests have less debris, which rules out choice **e.**

479. **c.** The fact that the Pyramid scheme is set up by a con artist suggests that the honest people who invest have been fooled. Choices **a** and **b** are contradicted in the passage. The paragraph says that the Pyramid scheme originated in the 1920s, but does not say it had its heyday then; thus choice **d** is incorrect. Choice **e** is a fact but is not mentioned in the passage.

480. **a.** This is expressed in the second sentence. Choice **b** is wrong because even though the people being investigated might be disreputable, the clients who have hired the investigator are not necessarily so. Choice **c** may be attractive, but the paragraph does not say that private investigators actually write detective fiction. The other choices are not in the passage.

481. **c.** The statement that it is difficult to create an accurate profile of a skyjacker comes immediately after a discussion of the extreme differences between skyjackers and their motives. Choice **a** is wrong because, although the paragraph says that the crime of skyjacking is unpredictable, it does not say that each individual skyjacker is unpredictable. The other choices are not in the passage.

SET 35 (Page 105)

482. **b.** If it is more expensive to run a medical practice in a large city than a small town, it would make sense for doctors to charge more in large cities. Choices **a**, **c**, and **e** are incorrect because the information in these statements is extraneous to the author's argument. Choice **d** is wrong because it supports, rather than refutes, the author's argument.

483. **e.** The passage states that "doctors in large cities make more money than doctors in small towns or rural areas." The speaker then assumes that if doctors all charge the same, they will all earn the same, but if doctors in large cities see more patients, they will still earn more money.

484. **a.** The argument is based on the idea that the government spends a great deal of money translating documents into different languages. Choices **b** and **e** make the argument somewhat weaker. Choice **c** offers no support for the argument. Choice **d** may offer some support, but choice **a** makes the argument much stronger.

485. **c.** If most people learn English within a short period of time, making English the official language is unnecessary.

486. **d.** The speaker maintains that to burn a flag is an act of freedom of speech, which is among the things the flag represents.

487. **a.** If an action is not included under freedom of speech, the speaker's main argument is incorrect.

488. **b.** This is the best choice because it relates to a situation where a proposed law would actually violate the part of the Constitution it is intended to protect.

SET 36 (Page 108)

489. **a.** Because the speaker is arguing that multiple guests should be allowed when fewer members are present, the purpose of the rule is to make sure members are not crowded by the presence of guests. There is no support for choices **b**, **c**, or **d**. Choice **e** is attractive, but it is not the best choice because there is no way the club could control which members would be at the club at any one time.

490. **c.** Joint pain caused by physical activity and that caused by arthritis may not respond the same way to medication.

491. **e.** This would indicate that the conditions of the football players and the speaker's mother are similar.

492. **c.** The speaker uses analogies to compare crawling with learning arithmetic and reading and to compare walking with using a computer. The speaker is making the point that, in both cases, a child needs to learn one before learning the other.

493. **e.** This evidence would back up the speaker's contention that young students should learn the basics before learning computers. Choices **a** and **d**, which are both about cost, would have no effect on the argument. Choices **b** and **c** are too vague.

494. **a.** If computers enhance the learning of arithmetic and reading, the speaker's argument is not as strong.

495. **b.** The speaker refers to the safety of children because most people are concerned about that. The speaker does not make a comparison (choice **a**). Choice **c** can be ruled out because the speaker does not give a specific number. Choices **d** and **e** are incorrect because the speaker doesn't give an account of any specific child, nor does he or she use any method of attack.

496. **e.** Since the speaker is basing the argument on the safety of children, if there are only a few accidents and none involved children, the argument is weaker.

SET 37 (Page 111)

497. b. Lars provides information that supports Frances's more general statements. Both agree that schools should spend money on educating children, not on providing breakfast. Choices **a**, **d**, and **e** are incorrect because they all imply that Frances and Lars are arguing in opposition to each other. Choice **c** can be ruled out because Lars's position does not give any outcomes.

498. d. Both speakers rely on the fact that schools do not traditionally have the responsibility for providing students with breakfast.

499. d. The speakers support their arguments in different ways, but both are concerned with whether sixteen-year-olds should continue to be allowed to receive drivers' licenses.

500. c. Quinn discusses the fairness of changing the law and raising the age at which one can receive a driver's license. Emotion (choice **b**) may be involved, but the argument relies on the fairness issue.

501. e. Dakota discusses the actualities of increased traffic and the decline in the teaching of drivers' education. She doesn't use statistics (choice **a**). Her argument is not emotion-filled, which rules out choice **b**. She doesn't mention fairness (choice **c**), and doesn't tell stories about specific situations (choice **d**).